Goodnight John-Boy

Goodnight John-Boy

A Celebration of an American Family and the Values That
Have Sustained Us Through Good Times and Bad

Earl Hamner & Ralph Giffin

CUMBERLAND HOUSE
NASHVILLE, TENNESSEE

Published by
  Cumberland House Publishing, Inc.
  431 Harding Industrial Drive
  Nashville, TN 37211-3160

Cover design: Gore Studio, Inc.
Text design: Mary Sanford

Library of Congress Cataloging-in-Publication Data
Hamner, Earl.
    Goodnight John-Boy : a celebration of an American family and the values that have sustained us through good times and bad / Earl Hamner & Ralph Giffin.
        p. cm.
Includes synopses of each episode and special of the television series The Waltons.
Includes bibliographical references (Internet resources) and index.
    ISBN 1-58182-298-7 (pbk. : alk. paper)
  1. Hamner, Earl. 2. Hamner, Earl—Family. 3. Hamner, Earl—Childhood and youth. 4. Authors, American—20th century—Biography. 5. Authors, American—20th century—Family relationships. 6. Television producers and directors—United States—Biography. 7. Blue Ridge Mountains Region—Social life and customs. 8. Rural families—Blue Ridge Mountains Region. 9. Virginia—Social life and customs. 10. Waltons (Television program) I. Giffin, Ralph, 1942– II. Title.
    PS3558.A456 Z468 2002
    813'.54—dc21

                                                                2002012120

Printed in Canada
3 4 5 6 7—08 07 06 05 04 03

*To the memory of my mother and father
And to my brothers and sisters:*

*Clifton Anderson Hamner (Deceased)
Marion Hamner Hawkes
Audrey Hamner
Paul Louis Hamner
Willard Harold Hamner (Deceased)
James Edmond Hamner
Nancy Hamner Jamerson*

*Thank you for your love and patience and for
sharing the good times we had growing up together.*

*Dedicated also to Woody Greenberg for his vision and
dedication to the people of Nelson County and
to Isis Ringrose for casting light in the darkness.*

EARL HAMNER

*To my loving wife, Judy,
who has blessed me with her
companionship, friendship, and love.
And to our four sons,
who have made us proud parents.
Thank you.*

RALPH GIFFIN

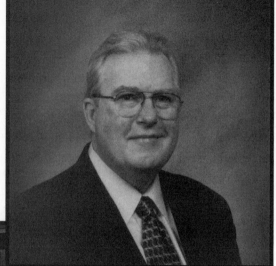

Earl Hamner *(below)* and Ralph Giffin *(right)*.

Contents

Foreword

"Say, 'Goodnight John-Boy'!"

I'VE BEEN HEARING IT FOR thirty years. In the street, in restaurants, yelled by hard-hatted workers on New York City construction sites, even over the phone from telemarketers who recognized my voice. Once, just before the first-act curtain of a Broadway play, it sailed from the back of the house, over the audience and landed delicately on the stage at my feet. It got the biggest laugh of the night.

One might consider this grounds for grudge-keeping, and I will admit that, for the first few years after I had left the cast of *The Waltons,* I was easily peeved. After all, I'd moved on, why couldn't millions of other Americans?

Well, that was the question, wasn't it? And the answer was that Earl Hamner had created such a vivid world, inhabited by such fully felt and richly observed characters—including himself—that the audience knew the real thing when they saw it, and it became for them the memory of an actual family.

Years later, it's easy to forget that *The Waltons* was a groundbreaking television series. A true ensemble drama that embraced all ages and defied the categories, being by turns funny, sad, serious, silly, and, at times, even exciting. It wasn't a show about super-lawyers, super-cops, or super-doctors. It wasn't even a show about people who always had jobs, let alone high-paying ones. It was just about a family trying to get along.

It's significant that *The Waltons* celebrated familism and healing during the tough times of the Great Depression, and that it was aired in the early seventies, a time when alienation, cynicism, Watergate, and the last years of the Vietnam War made its brand of family programming and deep-rooted optimism truly unique and even daring.

But those who thought of *The Waltons* as an escape into a perfect childhood that never was should remember that public issues such as book burning, prejudice, abuse, illiteracy, and poverty were frequently on the agenda, alongside the usual psychic struggles of growing up, growing old, and having a family. We weren't perfect, and Earl never wanted us to be.

What he wanted, I think, was truthfulness, and he gave all of us characters with which we could accomplish that. They were characters that evolved over time, people who grew and learned and changed. I remember my first pair of long pants, my first car, my first crush, and the surge of pride and joy at seeing my first story in print. I remember my brothers and sisters (Jon, Judy, Mary, Eric, Kami, and David) struggling to grow up, my mom and dad (the inestimable Michael Learned and Ralph Waite) on the journey of marriage and child rearing, and my grandparents (the irreplaceable Will Geer and

Richard Thomas at John-Boy's desk.

Ellen Corby) learning to grow old beautifully together. We were a work in progress, and because Earl was always open to suggestions about our characters' evolution we had a hand in our own fate.

The show was written in the authentic vein of the regional American short story, and because it came out of the author's personal history as so much great Southern writing does, we as actors were blessed with the tools of specificity. We were located historically, culturally, and linguistically in a real time and place. We didn't inhabit the generalized world of the American Television Planet—a place where no one I know has ever really lived.

It was a job worth doing, and it brought us all very close together. As our characters grew, so did we. I, personally, had a lot of growing up to do, and I did much of it on Stage 26 and the backlot of Burbank Studios in a place called "Walton Flats."

So, when I look back on the show, and remember Earl's mellow Virginia tenor saying, "When I was a young man, growing up on Walton's Mountain . . . ," I'm not remembering just John-Boy, I'm remembering my own youth as well, my own second family, my own journey into manhood. And we are so inextricably linked that, for me, I know it can never really be "Goodnight John-Boy" after all.

RICHARD THOMAS

Preface

*T*HE GREAT NORTH CAROLINA NOVELIST Thomas Wolfe said you can't go home again, but that has not been my experience. Even though home is far away, I go there often. Not to the hillside house in Studio City, California, where I live with my wife, but to my home as a youngster, some fifty years and three thousand miles away in the misted blue hills and valleys of Virginia's Blue Ridge Mountains.

My journey begins in Burbank at a movie studio. The fading light of day still tends the California gloaming. I drive through the back lot, a curious landscape: a Mexican settlement where water sprinkles in a deserted fountain, a Tibetan village where fake cherry blossoms cling to the tips of stage trees, a Midwestern village square where a silent bandstand echoes lost and forgotten march music, the darkened Western street where ghosts of movie gunslingers and cowboys seem to linger in the gathering dusk.

I come finally to a country lane, unpaved and bordered with green trees. I cross a mud puddle, follow the turning road, and I am "home" again. The house is a stage set, a shell, but a replica of the house I lived in as a child. It is a typical rural Virginia house, two-storied and white, built of clapboard. It rests in a wood. An old wooden barn stands nearby.

Evening winds fan white curtains at the windows and shadows loom in nonexistent rooms behind the façade. A porch extends the length of the house. A friendly wicker chair, a porch swing, and hanging baskets of flowers give the illusion of occupancy. I stop the car, turn off the engine, and listen to those creatures astir at that darkening hour. The crickets resume their chorus, the katydids resume their small metallic scream, and in memory I sense the sound of a screen door opening and hear again the voice of my mother calling to her children: "It's dark, children. Come home."

A stranger, distant and watching, I see myself and the children we were drift across the damp grass and go into the house. We were eight and I was the eldest. We all had red hair, and my father called us his "thoroughbreds." Standing together we made stairsteps, a row of lean, small-boned children who were living through a Depression but rarely knew what it was to be depressed. We knew we were loved because our mother and father loved each other and passed that love on to each of us.

This is the family I re-created in my books and on television, my brothers and sisters, my mother and father, my grandparents, as we were during the Depression years of the '30s. Sometimes watching the scene makes the memories of childhood return with such force and clarity that it brings tears to my eyes.

In memory there comes across the years the loveliest and most mystical sound I know—the night cry of a bobwhite. When I was growing up, after the chores were done in the evening, when it was time to rest, the whole family used to sit on the front porch. We would fall silent while my father would imitate the whistle of a bobwhite. In the distance a covey would answer. He would whistle again and the birds would answer, closer this time. Gradually his beguiling whistle would call the whole covey to the very edge of the porch. We thought my father possessed some kind of magic, and probably he did.

He is lost to us now, but some years ago when I grew lonesome for the sound of a

Earl tunes the radio that was used on the set of *The Waltons,* now on loan to the Walton Museum from the Smithsonian Institution.

bobwhite I was able to buy a pair, and I brought them home. They are not native to California, but somehow they made themselves at home and raised a family. I keep them in a pen near my home, and at night when I arrive home they recognize the sound of my car. They whistle to me. I whistle back to them and they answer.

Darkness falls, and once again a stranger before the façade of a building on the backlot at Warner Brothers, I hear the slap of the screen door closing, the children all safe inside to do homework, to listen to Edgar Bergen and Charlie McCarthy on the radio, and to prepare for bed.

After the last light is out they call to each other. *Goodnight, Cliff. Goodnight, Audrey. Goodnight, Marion. Goodnight, Mama. Goodnight, Daddy. Goodnight, Paul. Goodnight, Bill. Goodnight, Jim. Goodnight, Nancy. Goodnight, Earl.*

Their voices fade into time and memory. I am alone and I am refreshed and comforted. I ease the car away, past the sleeping Mexican square, the Tibetan village, and the Midwestern street, toward the California hillside where my wife waits for me, and when they hear my car pull into the driveway, the bobwhites will make their plaintive and mysterious call.

Earl Hamner, Richard Thomas, and Ralph Giffin on the *Waltons* set.

Acknowledgments

*T*HERE ARE SO MANY PEOPLE whose efforts made this book possible. I would like to express my love and appreciation first to my wife, Jane, and children, Scott and Caroline, who continued to love and support me although it seemed at times that my devotion was to another family. Among my friends at Lorimar, I thank Lee Rich for his recollection of how this all came about and Merv Adelson for his support. I owe endless gratitude to story editor Carol Evan McKeand, who saved my life about twice a day. Most of the folks at CBS are no longer there, but wherever you may be, much gratitude goes to Freddie Silverman, Ethel Winant, Bill Self, Perry Lafferty, and Tony Barr. I would also like to recognize the fans who kept us on the air when there appeared to be no hope for a future and who stayed with us all these years. A special thank you goes to Carolyn Grinnell, president of the Waltons International Fan Club, for her ceaseless devotion to the series and for all she has done on its behalf. I will always be indebted to Irene Porter for her nurturing the Waltons Friendship Society in Great Britain. I am deeply indebted to Woody Greenberg who had the vision to establish the Walton's Mountain Museum, and to the folks in my hometown who worked together to make Woody's dream a reality. Robert Brent Hall deserves special gratitude for bringing his professional designer talents to every aspect of the museum. I wish especially to thank Tom and Isis Ringrose, whose love and support has never wavered over the years. I am appreciative too to Dee-Davis Wells for her skillful and loving tenure as director of the Walton's Mountain Museum and to Valda Mulkey, who holds that position today with love and caring.

I am indebted too to my partner in the making of this book, Ralph Giffin, for his patience, attention to detail, creative input, rich resources, and even richer devotion to the series and what it stands for. Ralph's Web site, www.the-waltons.com, continues to be *the* source of information about the series, a meeting place for fans, a photograph gallery, and links to other pertinent Web sites.

Writing this book has been a labor of love, an excuse to look back on and relive a milestone in my life. One of the major reasons for the success *The Waltons* enjoyed was that each of you, writers, actors, directors, gave so unselfishly of your personal experience and talent and love. I wish to thank all of those friends and coworkers who have contributed so meaningfully to the series and to this book. There are many others who deserve to be named here, but who are not, simply because I could not track you down. This is especially true of the many different crews, painters, camerapeople, carpenters, soundpeople, editors, drivers, wranglers, designers, extras, costumers, makeup people, all of you who did the hard work, the exacting work, the very necessary work without which none of those words and faces would have gotten to the screen.

If I could have a wish come true it would be to walk onto Stage 26 one morning and find all of you there again, ready to film another episode, and to hear Harry Harris call, "Action! "

Goodnight John-Boy

The Hamner family in 1978: 1st row: Earl; 2nd row: Doris, Audrey;
3rd row: Willard, Paul, Jim, Marion, Nancy; 4th row: Cliff.

Chapter One

The Family

❧

W E WERE A TRADITIONAL VIRGINIA country family: my mother and father, my four sisters, my three brothers, and two sets of grandparents. I was the oldest of eight.

I was born on July 10, 1923, in Schuyler, Virginia. The village is in Nelson County in that part of the Blue Ridge referred to as the "Ragged Mountains." There's a guidebook to Virginia that was written during the Depression years under the supervision of the Works Progress Administration (WPA). In it Schuyler is described as "a tiny hamlet, which rises to mild hilarity on Saturday nights." If the observer was impressed with our exuberance on Saturday nights, he should have been around at one of our revival services when we atoned for our sins at the Baptist Church.

People will tell you there's a lot more sin around today than there was fifty years ago. I always remember something my grandmother Giannini said when I asked her about the difference between her generation and mine. "The only difference," she answered, "is that people today do on the front porch what we used to do out back."

When I was growing up in Nelson County, it seemed to me, and it does so now, that we had quite a good life.

We were an extended family living in a small white clapboard house. The house had been owned by the company that operated the soapstone mill that had brought the village into being. When the company closed it offered its company-owned houses for sale. My father bought ours for five hundred dollars.

We took our meals at a long wooden table in the kitchen, and I can still remember my father's pride when he looked around the table at his sons and daughters. We were slender of bone and lean. Some of us were freckled and some were not. Some had the brown eyes of our father and some had our

Left, Maternal grandparents Colonel Anderson Giannini and Ora Lee Giannini. *Below,* The Hamner home in Schuyler, Virginia. (Photo by Scott M. Hamner)

mother's green eyes, but on each of the children there was a stamp of grace in build and movement. It was this that our father meant when he said, as he often did, "Every one of my children is a thoroughbred."

It was the Great Depression, and the Alberene Stone Company, where my father worked as a machinist, closed. We were poor, but nobody ever bothered to tell us that. All we knew was that we suffered an absence of money. I have been accused of portraying the Depression years as too happy. It may have been severe for city people, but we were country people with country people's advantages.

It didn't bother us that we were poor. We were too occupied with day-to-day events. First came an end to winter and the melting of the icicles along the eves. Then March and time to climb Witt's Hill with kites made of brown wrapping paper and flown from string that had been collected for that purpose all winter long. The blossoming of the dogwood and redbud and forsythia told us that spring was back again.

Summer would come again, and with it dozens of cousins from Richmond and Petersburg. We were in awe of the cousins at first. They were "different," with their city ways and smart talk. They smoked cigarettes and knew wicked slang words, which we picked up and used out of hearing of our parents. At twilight we would catch fireflies, and after darkness fell we would sit on the front porch and listen to ghost stories told by our grandparents.

Paternal grandparents Walter Clifton Hamner and Susan Spencer Hamner.

At night there was always something to listen to on the radio. The whole family would gather around the old Atwater Kent table model and share *One Man's Family* (the nighttime soap of its day), or Charlie McCarthy ribbing Edgar Bergen, or Gene Autry singing "I'm Back in the Saddle Again," or one of President Roosevelt's Fireside Chats.

At least once every summer the whole clan, mothers and fathers, aunts, uncles, grandparents, and cousins would travel over to Uncle Benny Tapscott's farm in Buckingham County.

The barn behind the Hamner home. It is no longer standing. Just to the right of the barn was where my father set up a small sawmill after he lost his job in the Depression. (Photo by Scott W. Hamner)

We would feast on fried chicken and salty home-cured ham and old-fashioned potato salad and the sweetest iced tea you ever tasted. Later on we would all go to the springhouse and bring back chilled watermelon and cantaloupe. We would eat them on the grass and spit the seeds on the ground. Toward sundown someone would bring out a guitar. Grownups and young people alike would join in singing the old songs like "Down by the Old Mill Stream" and "Let Me Call You Sweetheart (I'm in Love With You)." Usually one of the uncles had gone down the road to Esmont and visited two ladies who made bootleg whiskey (they called it "the recipe"), and once they had shared it, they would put their arms around their brothers and cry with happiness. Finally, the uncles would pack their stern-eyed spouses and coveys of cranky children in their cars and we would all go home, not knowing that only when we had grown old would we appreciate that we had been the most fortunate of people.

Our parents were resourceful in feeding us. My father would go out at dawn and come back with bobwhite quail that my mother cooked with a dark brown gravy. There were bass and catfish in the Rockfish River, and always plenty of venison, both in and out of season. We kept pigs and always had a cow out grazing somewhere. I am probably the only writer in Hollywood who knows how to milk a cow, not that I get called on much to use that particular talent. I dream of the day when my agent will call and say: "Twentieth Century Fox is looking for a writer who can milk a cow." It won't happen.

Schuyler Baptist Church. (Photo by Scott M. Hamner)

With the coming of fall, summer's haze turned into crystal clear air. On a Sunday we would all pile into my father's Desoto and drive up to the recently opened Skyline Drive. Often we would simply stop the car and look out at the changeless beauty of those autumn leaves. The colors were visually intoxicating, and the brain reeled with colors that ranged from blood red to lemon yellow to lime green with all hues in between.

Back home we would gather chinquapins and black walnuts. And when the frost killed the vines we would gather the last of the green tomatoes, and the following day my mother's kitchen would be filled with the pungent aroma of green tomato relish.

Finally the long silent winter would be upon us. The first hint of Christmas would come with the arrival of the new mail-order catalog. We called it "the wish book," and while the great winter storms would rage across the Blue Ridge, we would gather, safe and warm around the long wooden table, gaze wistfully at each page of the wish book, and dream our Christmas dreams.

Charlottesville was twenty-six miles away, and a walk down its main street during the Christmas season was as awesome as a journey through Baghdad. Unlike the muddy country roads we knew, the town had paved streets with stoplights and streetcars and big window displays. We were foreign to all that sophistication and we showed it in our country clothes and country ways. We had little money to spend, but we did a lot of window-shopping with music provided by the Salvation Army playing a tinny version of "It Came upon the Midnight Clear."

We had picked out our Christmas tree in July. We found it while my brothers and sisters and I were picking blackberries up on Witt's Hill. It was a six-foot-tall cedar laden with pinecones and the pungent scent of evergreen. A week before Christmas we brought it into the house and set it up in a corner of the living room. It was as if we had captured some wild thing in the woods and tamed it. We strung lights on it and trimmed it with decorations, and its fragrant presence permeated the house.

Often Santa Claus would leave an orange, but more often there were gifts under the tree for each of us. Sometimes they were knitted gloves or a scarf and even, on occasion, a package of "sparklers" and "squibs," which were small red firecrackers with Chinese writing on the package they came in.

All during the school year, my mother supervised all eight of us children as we gathered around the long wooden kitchen table to do our homework. Then one by one we drifted off to bed and there, sometimes with snow falling outside, we would call goodnight to each other, then sleep in the knowledge that we were secure. We thought we lived in the best of all possible times.

After I moved to New York City, I learned that we had been "economically deprived." That we lived in a "depressed area" and that we suffered from a disease called "familism." Sociologists define *familism* as a type of social organization in which the family is considered more important than other social groups or the individual.

We didn't know we were afflicted with familism, we just thought we loved each other. Even today, with a highfaluting sociological name for it, I still prefer to call it love. We were demonstrative in our love, kissing and hugging a lot, and often we would drink a bit of the recipe and end up around the piano with our arms around each other singing the old Baptist hymns.

This was the family that inspired my books, which in turn were the basis for the motion picture *Spencer's Mountain* and the landmark television series *The Waltons*.

Beginning in 1972, the series was seen on Thursday nights on CBS by some fifty million viewers in the United States. It was also seen in Canada, Hong Kong, Japan, Australia, Fiji, Ireland, and Ecuador, to mention only a few of the countries where it was popular. In a single week, we received commendations from the Council of Christians and Jews, the Society of Southern Baptists, the Religious Public Relations Council of the Methodist Church, and the Church of Latter-day Saints. One Sunday we went beyond my wildest expectations. In a magazine called *Twin Circle*, which is the voice of the National Catholic Press, given equal space was a picture of the pope and a picture of the Walton family. I worried that we had gone too far!

In addition, we received six Emmy Awards, six Christopher Awards, the Golden Globe Award from the Foreign Press Association, the People's Choice Award, and the highest award given in the journalism field, the coveted Peabody Award from the University of Georgia.

The series ran for nine seasons on CBS. Several two-hour movies were filmed and today, thirty years after they were first seen on television, the Walton family is still very popular and beloved.

There must be a story there!

A Hamner Family Album

James

Audrey and Marion

Jim, Bill, and Paul

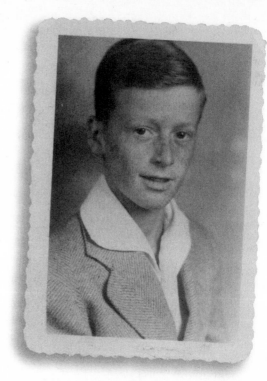

Bill

Paul

Nancy

Audrey

First photo of Earl, in lap of family friend.

At the museum (l–r): Jim, Paul, Audrey, Nancy, Marion, Earl.

A family photo: Earl Sr. (age ten) is at the far right, front row (holding duck).

Maternal grandparents Colonel Anderson Giannini and Ora Lee Giannini.

Doris and Jim

Clockwise from top right: Earl (home on army furlough), Paul, Jim, Bill, Cliff.

Doris Hamner

Jim, Nancy,
Marion (holding
baby), Bill,
and Doris

Earl and Jane Hamner

Earl growing up in Schuyler, Virginia, circa 1929.

Chapter Two

A Writer in the Family

❧

AS FAR BACK AS I can remember, I wanted to be a writer. My mother once told me that I was writing my numbers when I was two years old and reading by the time I was four. She was my first teacher, and when I started grade school I knew the first-grade primer by heart.

I kept a journal, and in it I wrote of whatever I found of interest during the day. Here is a page I came across not long ago:

> *Undated.* Today it rained and we all had to stay in the house. It wasn't much fun until Marion decided we would catch some birds. She got this old box from Luke Snead and set it up in the yard under the maple tree. She propped up one end of the box with a stick and tied a string to one end of the stick so she could pull it from where we were all hiding by the kitchen door. Under the box she put some stale bread and then we all waited and watched for the birds to come.
>
> A cardinal showed up first. He saw the bread but he wouldn't go in there. Once he kind of poked his head in and Bill kept hollering for Marion to pull the string and she kept hollering for him to shut up. Then the cardinal flew off and Marion blamed Bill and he started crying and saying curse words and Mama came in and said, "Lord, what are y'all children up to now?"
>
> Marion said we were catching birds and Mama said that was all right as long as we didn't kill any and let them go after we looked at them.
>
> After a while about a million gold finches showed up and swarmed around the box, just showed up out of nowhere. They walked around the box for a while just looking at the bread crumbs. After a while one of them walked in.
>
> Bill yelled "Pull the string!" Marion pulled it, but the goldfinch flew away before the box fell on him. We watched him fly to the crab apple tree and the rest of them were roosting up there too.
>
> Marion got mad and there was a fight between her and Bill and while I was trying to break up the fight all the birds flew away.

Earl Hamner Sr. relaxing in the yard.

Over the years I have lost most of those journals, but I think even then I was practicing to be a writer.

When I was six I wrote a poem called "My Dog." It is a Christmas poem and tells how on Christmas morning I wear my new blue sweater while I pull my six puppies around in my new red wagon. My mother sent the poem to the children's page of the *Richmond Times Dispatch* and they published it!

There was no questioning my writing career after that. At six I had become a published writer! I also discovered that writing is about 10 percent fact and 90 percent imagination. I discovered also that I could scare the hell out of my daddy because I did not have a new red wagon; neither did I have a blue sweater nor six puppies! I had made them up! This worried my father. What kind of child have we got here? Where did such craziness come from? I think he worried about my having an ambition that seemed strange and unrealistic. He wanted a more sure way of my making a living for myself. A trade was the answer, and he intended to teach me the mechanics trade when the time came. He worried about this over the years, and it wasn't until I invited him to the premiere of one of my movies at New York's Radio City Music Hall that I believe I set his mind at ease.

But Radio City Music Hall was a long way off in those days. As promising as my first effort had been, there was little hope for my future as a writer. Writers were people with names like Henry Wadsworth Longfellow and William Makepeace Thackeray or Oliver Wendell Holmes. They lived in distant and exotic places like London, New York, or Boston. How presumptuous it was for a boy named Earl Hamner from the backwoods of the Blue Ridge Mountains to aspire to join that illustrious group. The whole idea was laughable. The obstacles were insurmountable. Still I kept my journal and I wrote in it each day, and I dreamed of the day when I would share my thoughts and my feelings and my world with my readers.

I graduated from Schuyler High School in 1939. The pinched and barren years of the Great Depression were slipping into history, but another event—World War II—was already hovering on the horizon. Winning a scholarship allowed me to enter the University of Richmond in 1940. The scholarship covered some items, such as tuition, but I still needed a place to live and food to eat, and three of my father's sisters were generous enough to take me into their home not far from the university.

The first time I ever actually confessed my secret intention of being a writer was to my aunt Nora Spencer Hamner. She was my father's oldest sister and a remarkable woman. None of the family had ever attended college at that time, but Nora had graduated from the Medical College of Virginia as a nurse. She then returned to our mountains where she "gave something back," as the saying goes. There was no doctor in the backwoods of our area in those days. Medical attention was available at the clinic of the University of

Virginia Hospital in Charlottesville. Even so, many of the mountain people were so ignorant of what was available they did not avail themselves of the care they could have received. Nora became "the nurse on horseback," and she would set out for weeks at a time with a small bag of medicines and instruments. She visited the hills and hollows, many of them occupied by extremely xenophobic hill folk. She became friend, doctor, midwife, minister, and on one occasion undertaker to the folks who had grown to trust her.

It was many years later now and Nora had become executive secretary of the Richmond Tuberculosis Association. It was September and she was driving her "woody" station wagon from Schuyler to Richmond. Aunt Nora had spent the weekend up at her cottage just off the Blue Ridge Parkway. I had spent the weekend at home up in the country, and she had stopped by to give me a ride back to Richmond. Nora smoked Chesterfield cigarettes. They normally had a strong, acrid aroma, but the cool autumn air diluted the smoke and it made the air faintly scented and pleasant.

"What are you going to do with your life?" she asked as we drove along the beautiful old River Road that wound its way alongside the James River from Scottsville to Richmond.

I decided to confess. I had held the secret inside for much too long.

"I'm going to be a writer," I said. I looked at her to see how she would take this news.

"What are you going to write about?" she asked.

I had never thought about

Earl receiving an honorary degree from the University of Richmond.

The University of Richmond, model for Boatwright University.

that, and when I admitted it I realized it was an extremely weak answer. Here was the hope of the Hamner clan, the first Hamner to attend college, the one who might lead his brothers and sisters out of the backwoods and into the mainstream of American life, and HE DIDN'T KNOW WHAT HE WAS GOING TO WRITE ABOUT!

"Writers have messages. They have things to say," observed Aunt Nora. I think she meant it as guidance, but I felt defeated, my confidence and my ambition deflated.

I did have a story in mind. It was about a boy from the hills who falls in love with a girl who visits from New York. It was based loosely on my feelings for a girl who used to visit Schuyler each summer. The story did not seem substantial enough to tell Aunt Nora so I kept my mouth shut and suffered the defeat of being a writer who had no idea what he had to say.

At the University of Richmond I devoured English and American literature courses and flunked calculus. I took my first course in writing and submitted my hill boy/city girl story to Professor Ball. I did not tell him I intended to be the next William Faulkner or Thomas Wolfe. I was so sure the story was perfect in every way and that it would secure me a place in literary history, that the professor would want me to send it off to the *New Yorker* at once. He read the story, and when he returned it he had written such negative notes in the margin that I was stunned. Looking back, I cannot blame Professor Ball. The story took place almost entirely in New York City and the girl's family lived in a penthouse and went to nightclubs. I knew nothing about rich New Yorkers, had no idea what a penthouse looked like, and had never been in a nightclub! The experience was the first of a series of grave setbacks, and it was several weeks before I could bring myself to try to write again.

My college days were interrupted when I was conscripted into the army for service in World War II. Throughout the war I wrote stories. I kept a pen and a pad of paper with me and wrote constantly. Even after a thirty-mile hike up Agony Hill at

Earl home from Camp Lee Induction Center.

Fort Knox, Kentucky, I wrote. At Fort Leonard Wood in Missouri, after a day of being stuck in the mud while driving a six-by-six truck, I wrote. I kept writing material with me overseas. I remember a Replacement Depot in northern England near a little town called Nantwich. Daylight lasted until almost eleven o'clock, and I would sit at a table outside a pub and drink warm beer from a pitcher and scribble my stories. I remember writing as long as the light would allow from the hedgerows of Normandy with the rumble of gunfire only a few miles away. And finally in Paris, where I was fortunate enough to be stationed for two years, I worked in an office and had

Earl as a student at the College of Music of the University of Cincinnati, Ohio.

the luxury of access to a typewriter. I mailed those stories off to magazines and the editors mailed them right back. They were printed rejection slips usually. "This story does not suit our needs." "No manuscript accepted unless submitted through an agent." "Returned unread." That is the rejection that hurt my feelings the most.

After the war, I was able to take advantage of the GI Bill and attend the College of Music of Cincinnati, a branch of the University of Cincinnati. There I studied radio writing, and for the first time in my life I got paid for something I had written by selling a script to *The Dr. Christian Show.*

Earl at his desk at
NBC in 1952.

That sale was beneficial. It brought me to the attention of Bernie Madison, the writing supervisor at WLW, Cincinnati's premier radio station, and I went straight from college to a job on the writing staff. We wrote everything! There was a wonderful show called *Builders of Destiny* on which we dramatized the lives of notable people living in the listening area. I enjoyed writing for a children's show called *The Land of the Giants* and even ended up as narrator on the show. Being an old country boy with a love for country music, I was a natural to write *The Ernie Lee Show.* Rosemary Clooney, Red Skelton, Rod Serling, Doris Day, and Fats Waller had all worked there from time to time.

In 1949, just as John-Boy does on the series, I decided to try my luck in New York. There I met and was hired by one of the finest men I have ever known. His name was Van Woodward, another WLW alumnus. He became my friend and mentor. Soon after he hired me, Van realized I needed grooming and coaching if I was to measure up to the demands of a network position. When I handed my first script to him, Van said, "Cuz, it needs work." We worked on the script right through the night, and by sunup Van had taught me so many ins and outs of the writing profession that I was able to measure up.

The job was a dream. I had an office in Suite 211 of the RCA Building. My room overlooked Forty-ninth Street and was directly across from the dressing room of the Radio City Rockettes. I am not a voyeur, but it was definitely a challenge to keep my eyes on my typewriter when those gorgeous, young, long-legged dancers would spill from the stage into their dressing room and change for their next number. They were usually so rushed that they gave little thought to their privacy, and after a bit I realized that they weren't above showing off their generous gifts.

The mood of the office was relaxed, and the other writers were "characters." One of them was so phobic about elevators that he could only go a few floors at a time before getting off to "rest." Another could only write in the nude. Thoughtfully he kept his office door closed while he wrote. One gifted writer named Ernest Kinoy was such a fast writer that he could come in late on a Friday afternoon. His typewriter would go at a furious rate for two hours during which time he would write the one required script of the week.

I loved the job, and I loved writing for radio. On *The Waltons*, John-Boy becomes a newscaster, and for a while I did work for the

Cliff, Jim, Earl Hamner Sr., Paul, and Bill with his bride at their wedding reception.

Today Show and for an NBC documentary unit called "Wide Wide World," but most of the time I was assigned to radio drama. One week I would write an adaptation of a classic for *NBC Theater*. The following week I might produce a special in which some noted author would read from his or her works. Another time I would write a love story. For a while I was assigned to write continuity for one of the grande dames of the theater, Miss Eva Le Gallienne, who was hostess of an hourlong quality drama.

And then came television. The medium appealed to me from the first time I saw it. I wanted to be a part of it, but I encountered an unexpected obstacle.

I went to see television producers, but at every turn I was told, "You're a radio writer. You write for the ear. Television requires writers who know how to write for the ear and the eye!" "I can do that," I would insist, but nobody believed me. Finally, desperate, I approached a friend named Mark Smith. Mark was the story editor of *The United States Steel Hour,* which was produced by the *Theater Guild on the Air.* I knew Mark because he was married to one of my fellow staff writers, Claris Ross Smith.

I asked Mark to give me the same assignment he might hand out to his best writer. If it was an original idea he would tell me the same idea. If it was an adaptation he would give me a copy of what was to be adapted. Whatever the assignment, I promised him that I would accept it and demand no pay, no strings attached, except that he had to promise he would read my script. I guaranteed that my script would be better than that of his best writer.

Mark thought for a moment and then said, "I won't accept your dare. But I admire your arrogance, and I'm going to give you an assignment." I don't remember the story clearly. It was something about an oil well. While the owner drills he dreams of becoming rich and then discovers there is no oil in the well. But he realizes that achieving wealth can also mean realizing the richness of every-day life. Mark liked my script and it was produced.

From that day on I never had to worry about getting work in television in New York, and I had entered what was to become known as the "Golden Age of Television." Most of it was written and produced in New York City, but the advertising industry gradually took it over and it quickly lost its "golden" aura. What happened was that advertisers and producers discovered that the bulk of television—game shows, sitcoms, and musicals—could be produced more quickly and for less money on film, and so the industry moved to the West Coast.

By the end of the fifties there was hardly any dramatic television left in New York, so I decided to move west and try my hand at writing for films. My wife and I packed our two children, two cocker spaniels, and a Virginia land turtle into a train and headed for Hollywood.

And there I ran into the same rigid thinking I had encountered back in New York when I had tried to make the switch from radio to TV.

"You haven't written for film," I was told repeatedly by the Hollywood producers. It was as if writing for film were something that had to be breathed in with the smog, as if there were something so mystifying about writing film that it could not be mastered by an ordinary mortal.

And for six months I was unable to find work. It did not matter that I had made a living for the last ten years as a staff writer at NBC. It did not matter that I had published two books. What mattered was that I had not written for film.

I remembered that I had met Rod Serling back in 1949 when we were both writers on *The Dr. Christian Show.* I had been a fan of his creation, *The Twilight Zone,* and had often thought of stories that would be appropriate for the series. I wrote two such stories and submitted them to Rod. He responded quickly with a note that said he liked the stories but they were chosen by a committee and that he was submitting them to the committee. I was convinced that Rod hated the stories and that I would never hear from him again.

I was wrong. A man named Buck Houghton, the producer of *The Twilight Zone,* called and said, "We like your stories. We want to buy both of them."

To this day I can remember the elation and the relief, for we had long since reached the end of our financial rope.

"We have heard that you don't write film," continued Buck, and my heart sank. "So would you like to write them up like little plays?"

"I would like to write them up as television scripts," I answered. I did, and I never had to look for work in Hollywood again.

What we laughingly called "The Hamner Fortune" was replenished by the sale to *The Twilight Zone* and soon after that we had another windfall. My book *Spencer's Mountain* was bought by Warner Brothers.

Chapter Three

Spencer's Mountain

❧

HAVE NEVER BEEN SUPERSTITIOUS, nor have I put much store in astrology or dreams and portents, the predictions of stargazers or fortunetellers. Yet, the following mysterious thing happened to me:

When my family and I first moved to California, it took me a long time to find work and we quickly ran short of money. We were renting a small house in Studio City. There was no room for an office and no money to rent one, so I wrote in a corner of the garage, which looked out on the street. While trying to find a job in the industry I spent my spare time working on an autobiographical novel. The garage, of course, was not air-conditioned, so I kept the rollup door open most of the time.

Passersby were curious about the sight of a man typing away in a garage, and I was interested in them as well. I was fascinated by all those who passed by, but none so much as Peter the Hermit. I learned in time that Peter lived in the guest house of a movie actor who lived a few blocks away. Occasionally he appeared in films as an extra. Residents of the area will remember the little pink-faced man with the long white hair. He always dressed in white and frequently rode by on a mule. He was a friendly old fellow, and if the garage door was open he never failed to stop and say hello.

I had a picture of a family friend, Susie Salter, stapled to my bulletin board above the desk where I worked. She had introduced me to the girl who was to become my wife. Peter stopped once to admire the picture of the pretty woman and asked her name. I told him, and he responded that she was born on September 8. I didn't remember Susie's birthday, but later when I asked my wife she gave me the exact same date Peter had said. Just one of those things, I thought. A long shot. Something that just couldn't be explained. And then I forgot about the incident.

The original book jacket for *Spencer's Mountain*.

Later, I was at my typewriter and Peter peered in and asked what I was up to and I told him I was writing a book. Without hesitation he said, "Use the word *mountain* in the title and it will be a big success."

I had a different working title for the book, but my editor, Jim Silberman, came up with the title *Spencer's Mountain*! He was right, and so was Peter the Hermit! The book was most successful.

The inspiration for the book came from a dream my father had. He often said, and he really believed, that someday he would build a house for my mother with his own hands. "It will be a white house with green shutters, and it will sit on the top of the mountain. There'll be a big window where your mama can look out on the valley, and a porch all the way across the front where we can all sit and rest of an evening when the work's all done."

My father never even got to start the house. As he used to say, "The sun goes down too soon for a poor man." Still the dream of the house was a promise that sustained the whole family. We believed it would be built and that we would live there. It was only a matter of time.

In my novel, entwined with my father's dream, I devised a plot about a bright boy from a big backwoods family who dreamed of going to college, the first in his family to do so. But in order for the son to pursue his dream, the father must sacrifice his, give up on the house he has started to build, and sell the mountain to send his son off to college.

The novel attracted attention even before publication. A copy of the manuscript was sent to the gifted author Harper Lee, who wrote *To Kill a Mockingbird*. Miss Lee gave the book a glowing endorsement: "It is so easy to create a villain or an eccentric. It is so hard to

The German translation of *Spencer's Mountain*.

create good people and make them unforgettable. Each character in *Spencer's Mountain* is memorable, because life itself flows in abundance from each. One finds pure joy in reading, for a change, a positive statement on the potentialities of man." It was generous of Miss Lee and I am grateful to her for always.

Spencer's Mountain was published in 1961 by the Dial Press. It came out to uniformly good reviews. A typical one came from the *Chicago Tribune*: "A wonderful tale of life in the Old Dominion state. Like a breath of air blowing over snowy meadows, over sweet-scented pine-lands, it is never far from the roots of life, never distant from the heart strings of the emotions."

The book made the *New York Times* bestseller list. It was selected to be a *Reader's Digest* condensed book. My agent, Don Congdon, sold the foreign rights to France, England, Spain, Japan, Germany, Denmark, and Sweden. Dell reprinted it in a paperback edition. It was issued on tape as an audio book.

And then President John F. Kennedy selected the book to be included in a library that he was assembling to be presented to the heads of state of a hundred countries around the world. The collection of books was supposed to represent a cross section of the best of American life. I am still proud of that! Sometimes when we are in London and go past Buckingham Palace, I'll nudge my wife, Jane, and say, "I wonder if *she's* read it yet."

One of the conditions of the sale to Warner Brothers was that the director was to write the script. I was disappointed, but I was in no position to bargain. The Warner Brothers spokesperson did promise that I could read the script before it was filmed and would be granted the right to make suggestions.

I read the script with increasing panic. I had stressed in the publicity that the characters were based very directly on my own family. My mother and father were proud, upstanding, strait-laced, virtuous Baptists. Imagine my distress to find the father in the script saying to his wife: "Reminds me of when we used to sneak off in the bushes when we were courting." My mother would have died!

I managed to get them to remove that line and several others that would have been embarrassing to my parents, but still some gross dialogue and vulgar situations were kept in.

There was one dialogue exchange, which went as follows:

Voluptuous girl: Let's look up words in the dictionary.
Clay-Boy: What word?
Voluptuous girl: Friction.
Clay-Boy: (Finds word and reads) "Friction. The movement
of two bodies against each other."
Voluptuous girl: Friction me for ten seconds.

Maureen O'Hara and
Henry Fonda with
their family in
Spencer's Mountain.

I asked that the tasteless exchange be removed on the grounds that
what should be an act of love would be reduced to "friction."
The dialogue stayed in the film.
When the casting was announced I was thrilled. Henry Fonda

had agreed to play the father. Maureen O'Hara was persuaded to play the role of Olivia. James MacArthur (*Hawaii Five-O*) would play Clay-Boy. Donald Crisp (*How Green Was My Valley*) and Wally Cox (*Mr. Peepers* from television) were to appear in minor roles.

Henry Fonda told me later that he had accepted the role after he had read the book, and that when he read the script he was sorry he had already signed the contract. Still he brought depth and dignity to the role. Miss O'Hara brought charm and beauty and dimension to the role of the mother. Jim MacArthur, with rippling muscles and bare chest, was appealing in spite of appearing to be in his late twenties while playing a sixteen-year-old boy. As one writer described it, "The whole family became friskier!"

The filming proceeded in Jackson Hole, Wyoming, and it was at this point that the film got out of proportion to the book. Everything got big—really big! Instead of the gentle old Blue Ridge Mountains where the story was set, the film was shot in the magnificent Grand Tetons. Really, really big. The surroundings were magnificent but totally out of keeping with the modest story and the humble, folksy characters. The movie was filmed in, what else, Technicolor and Panavision, and on top of its other excesses the score was written by Max Steiner, who had also composed the music for *Gone With the Wind*! Big! Really big! When it came time for its world premiere, nothing would do but the most colossal movie theater in the world: Radio City Music Hall!

Don't get me wrong. I loved much about the movie. Whole convoys of Virginians came up to New York to the premiere. I was able to demonstrate to my father that I really could make a decent living for my family, and we all had a grand time visiting New York.

On the whole the reviews were kind. One who wasn't so kind was Judith Crist, who wrote in the *New York Herald Tribune*, ". . . the folks seem to spend most of their time either prayin' or playin' around with propagation in view."

My parents weren't upset by the "playin' around," but they never knew that I had saved them from a sullied reputation they did not deserve. Many people enjoy the movie still and watch it late at night on cable. I recently saw it on American Movie Classics and was moved by several scenes. I just wish it had all been done on a much smaller scale and with a little more sensitivity.

However the film came out, it marked the beginning of my family's journey to Hollywood, where the Hamners became the Spencers and were eventually to become the Waltons.

Warner Brothers had paid me a decent sum for the rights to the book, but it all went to the government in taxes, so I was soon back at labor. During the '60s I was a freelance writer and wrote for everything from *Nanny and the Professor* to *Wagon Train*. I wrote for a series that has been forgotten except for the few of us who worked on it called *It's a Man's World*.

Producers Fred Brogger and Jim Franciscus hired me to write an adaptation of the classic children's book *Heidi*. It was a most pleasant experience. Fred and I scouted locations in the Swiss Alps and near Saint Moritz, and we found a dream of a location for the grandfather's hut. To make the experience even more memorable, Fred and Jim were able to hire the gifted director Delbert Mann. Patricia Neal once described Del as "a heavenly man." She might just as well have said "a heavenly director." Del was a dominant director during television's golden age. His credits are distinguished and countless, but the mention of his name always brings to mind the Award-winning television play *Marty*.

Delbert assembled a remarkable cast, including Jean Simmons, Sir Michael Redgrave, Walter Slezak, Maximilian Schell, and the remarkable Jennifer Edwards, the nine-year-old daughter of director Blake Edwards, to play Heidi.

The show was special for me in many ways. Jane and I had written the words to a song for Heidi to sing. It was called simply "Heidi's Song." In the book, and in my script, Heidi has been bumped from place to place without any real home, so we tried to express her longing for a place of her own. John Williams set the words to music, Jenny Edwards sang it, and it added greatly to the poignant nature of the piece.

And then the show was aired.

Preceding the broadcast on NBC was a football game between the New York Jets and the Oakland Raiders. The game had one minute and fifteen seconds to go when *Heidi* was scheduled to begin. NBC made the fateful decision to preempt the rest of the game. *Heidi* started on time but caused the football fans to miss two touchdowns and two extra points, which completely changed the outcome of the game.

Anger is a mild word to describe the ire of the fans. They swamped NBC's switchboard. According to the Associated Press: "The mistake led to such a deluge of telephone calls that the fuses in the switchboard blew out."

Television critic Harriet Van Horne had an interesting footnote: "To exploit this little tempest, a full-page ad quoting the critics' tributes to *Heidi* included a wistful statement from Jets star Joe Namath: 'I didn't get a chance to see it, but I hear it was great,' said Joe."

I wrote for *CBS Playhouse* and *The Twilight Zone,* and I even wrote three movies. I am probably most proud of my adaptation of *Charlotte's Web,* but I also enjoyed writing *Where the Lilies Bloom* because it gave me the chance to work with the distinguished film producer Robert Radnitz. During this time I even wrote a movie that has become a cult classic, a ridiculous one I admit, but I still watch *Palm Springs Weekend* for laughs.

And while I was writing film and television, in my spare time I was working on a sequel to *Spencer's Mountain* called *The Homecoming.* It was published by Random House in spring of 1961. The prophecy of Peter the Hermit was about to be fulfilled again.

Chapter Four

The Homecoming
❧

*T*HE *HOMECOMING* WAS A SEQUEL to *Spencer's Mountain*. Like most of my writing, it was inspired by a family event.

In the early thirties the mill on which Schuyler depended had to close. The Depression was at its height. Money was scarce. Jobs were hard to find. My father found work in Waynesboro, which was fifty miles away. He could only be with us on weekends. He did not own a car, so he would take the bus to Hickory Creek on Route 29. From there he would hitchhike or walk the rest of the way home.

On Christmas Eve of 1933, snow had begun early in the morning. All day the small flakes had fallen steadily along with tiny pellets of sleet. By nightfall, every road had turned into a slippery and treacherous mess. My mother started to worry even before darkness fell, but as the snow became deeper and deeper we children joined her in concern over our father.

My mother tried to keep us busy. The girls gave the house an extra dusting and shine and helped her make her applesauce cake. I milked Chance while the younger brothers brought in stove wood.

My mother was an optimist, never one to give up, but her hopes diminished as the hours went by. Around nine o'clock she sent me out to look for our father. I started at the pool hall, the only establishment in the village that served beer and was a kind of private club for the men. No children were allowed and no decent woman ever set foot in the place. None of the pool players had seen my father. I asked at the local merchandise store and at neighbors' houses and walked as far as the snow would allow before I turned back.

Finally, when he had not arrived by midnight we went to our beds, but I doubt that even the youngest child had gone to sleep.

Suddenly a terrifying noise shook the house!

The noise was terrifying, a crash on the roof in the middle of the night. It could have been a meteor, an earthquake, a tornado! The situation was even more alarming because our father was not home.

"Mama!" the children shrieked as they jumped out of their beds.

"What is it, Mama?" I called.

"I don't know," our mother answered from our parents' room. My brothers and sisters and I crept down the stairway and joined our mother as she came out of her room, and we ran down the hall.

And there in the kitchen, just coming in the kitchen door, shaking the snow from his shoulders, a mischievous grin on his face, was my father. He carried a large burlap bag.

We all rushed to embrace him, vastly relieved that he was safe and home. He had missed the last bus from Waynesboro, had hitch-

My grandfather used to say that nobody owns a mountain; but getting born, and living, and dying in its shadow, we loved Walton's Mountain and felt it was ours. The Walton family had endured in that part of the Blue Ridge for over two hundred years. A short time in the history of a mountain. Still, our roots had grown deep in its earth.

When I was growing up there with my brothers and sisters, I was certain that no one on Earth had quite so good a life. I was fifteen and growing at an alarming rate. Each morning I woke convinced that I had added another inch to my height while I slept. I was trying hard to fill my father's shoes that winter. We were in the middle of the Depression, and the mill, on which our village depended, had closed. My father had found work in a town fifty miles away and he could only be with us on weekends. On Christmas Eve, early in the afternoon, we had already started looking forward to his homecoming. . . .

PRELUDE TO *The Homecoming*, CBS TELEVISION

Goodnight John-Boy

The book jacket for *The Homecoming.*

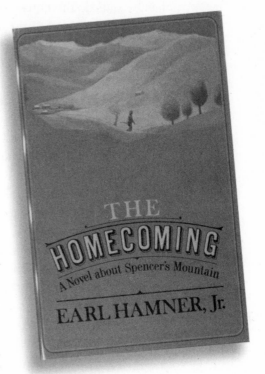

hiked to Hickory Creek. From there he had walked six miles through blinding snow. Our relief quickly turned to curiosity about the sack he was carrying, but first he wanted to explain the noise we had heard on the roof.

My mother warmed his supper while we gathered around the table to listen.

"I was just coming up the front walk," he explained. "When I looked up I saw something land on the roof. Looked like some kind of old sleigh pulled by funny little animals, about the size of a calf, had horns."

"Reindeer," breathed one of the younger children.

"Could have been," he said. "Funny-looking little old man jumped out of the thing. Big-bellied old fart, had on a red suit with a white collar and a bag of stuff over his shoulder!"

"Santa Claus!" said another child in a hushed voice.

"Nobody I knew, so I threw a rock at him, scared him so bad he slipped off the roof."

"I hope you didn't kill him," said another child reproachfully.

"Hell, no," breathed Daddy. "He bounced. On the second bounce I grabbed that bag away from him and there it is right there!"

"What you reckon is in it?" asked one of the children.

"Be damned if I know," he said. "Let's open it and see."

And then my father opened the bag of gifts and out came wonder—presents for each and every one of us, practical, well-chosen, store-bought, wondrous Christmas presents!

My father, a true dramatist, repeated this performance with variations year after year. Sometimes he pretended to hear footsteps outside the house. He would go outside to investigate and return with a bag of Christmas candy, which he claimed had been specially delivered by an elf. At other times Mrs. Claus had dropped things off because the old man was sick! If I ever wondered where I got the imagination it takes to be a writer, I didn't have to look far!

I had always intended to write about that Christmas Eve as a short story, but when I started writing the short story became a novella. The editor I had come to revere, Jim Silberman, who had edited *Spencer's Mountain,* was still at Random House and he published the book.

I loved the book with its forest green cover and a drawing that at first glance seemed to be of a mountain covered with snow. But when the drawing is examined more closely, the figure of a boy becomes discernible. He is moving toward some fir trees, ax in hand. Beyond him in the distance is a home with icicles dripping from the edge of the roof and farther off a cluster of houses marks the center of a small hamlet.

The book received good reviews, had a modest sale and was bought by the Reader's Digest Condensed Book Club. My New York agent, Don Congdon, started a significant chain of events by sending a copy of the book to his Hollywood colleague, Malcolm Stewart, a friend who was an agent at the International Famous Agency.

Malcolm asked if he might submit the galleys to a relatively new production company called Lorimar. Lorimar was a partnership between Lee Rich, a former advertising executive, and Merv Adelson, a businessman and investor. They worked out of an office on Rodeo Drive in Beverly Hills. Lee Rich was president of the company, Merv Adelson, chariman of the board. Around them they had gathered people with good solid backgrounds in the industry. Bob Jacks, who had substantial credits as a film producer at Twentieth Century Fox, had been hired as a producer. Carol Evan McKeand, a novelist and television producer, had come aboard to develop new projects. And Roseblanche Schwartz, the secretary, steered the ship! It is much to the credit of Lorimar that they chose top people in their fields to bring their projects to life.

When the book arrived at Lorimar, Lee Rich read it, liked it, and sent it to CBS.

Joanne Brough was executive story editor of the CBS Network at that time. It was her job to read and critique every project submitted to the network. Eventually *The Homecoming* arrived at her desk. In her report Joanne wrote:

> It is obviously slanted toward Christmas Eve audiences and I believe it could potentially become a classic. It is filled with rich characterization and the warm family relationship is beautifully portrayed. It has something of the feel of *A Christmas Memory,* but this would be a more important film.

On the East Coast, Phil Capice, vice president of specials and movies at CBS, read the book and commissioned it to be a film. He mentioned his enthusiasm to Freddie Silverman, vice president in charge of programs, and Freddie agreed. Lorimar was told to proceed with a script. I met with the Lorimar people and they asked me to write the two-hour screenplay. It was my pleasure. I had adapted other writers' work to film, and I had always been guided by respect for the original work, to keep the integrity of the author's vision and to be faithful to the original work. Now it was my turn to be faithful to my own work!

Script in hand, we began casting the film under the watchful eye of Ethel Winant, head of casting at CBS, and Pam Polifroni, the casting agent we hired to cast the film. We began looking for an actor to fill the important role of Clay-Boy.

I had seen Richard Thomas in a movie called *Red Sky at Morning.* Richard played the role of a young Southern boy who comes of age at the same time his father leaves the family behind to fight in the navy in World War II. Claire Bloom played the mother, Richard Crenna was the father, Desi Arnaz Jr. was his friend, and Richard was sensational as the young man. I knew he would make an unforgettable Clay-Boy.

We approached Richard, but he was not anxious to make a television film. His movie career was on the rise and more film roles were just around the corner. But when he read the script he liked it and he took the job. Richard brought to the role a rich background in the theater. He had been a working actor since his appearance on Broadway in *Sunrise at Campobello* when he was seven years old. In between TV and stage work he managed to

Left, Patricia Neal and Andrew Duggan. *Below,* The Waltons celebrate Christmas in *The Homecoming.*

attend Columbia University. He brought sensitivity and respect to the role, and I have often said that Richard made a better John-Boy than I did!

Key to the success of the film was the choice of Fielder Cook to direct. I was not the only Virginian involved in the film production of *The Homecoming*. Fielder is from an old Shenandoah Valley family. He has a distinguished career in movies and television, and his accomplishments go back to the golden years of television. Fielder is a striking figure. He often wears an ice cream suit and a planter's hat. He is the kind of person who attracts glances and whispers of "Who is he?" when on his way to his table at restaurants.

Once Fielder was on board and our star was selected, we began assembling a crew, and again Lorimar extended itself and hired such notable people as Russ Metty, an Oscar-winning cinematographer; Ed Graves, art director; Patty Norris, costume designer; and the aristocrats of film editing, Marge and Gene Fowler. In addition to their considerable talents, the Fowlers were both from distinguished writing families: Gene was the son of the great novelist Gene

Patricia Neal and Richard Thomas in *The Homecoming*.

Fowler, and Marge was the daughter of the esteemed screenwriter Nunnally Johnson.

We continued casting the rest of the movie. A script was sent to Patricia Neal at her home in Great Missenden, a suburb of London. It was the first acting job Patricia considered after suffering a severe stroke. She accepted the job. If we had any concern about her ability to do the role we need not have worried. She arrived from London with every word of the script memorized!

Ellen Corby was born in Racine, Wisconsin, as Ellen Hansen. She and her mother (known as Buddy) arrived in Hollywood in the thirties. Ellen took a job as a script girl, but her heart was in acting. Once she turned to acting she appeared in more than one hundred

Top, Richard Thomas as John-Boy and Patricia Neal as Olivia. *Above,* Ellen Corby and Edgar Bergen as Grandma and Grandpa Walton.

movies, including *It's a Wonderful Life* and *Shane.* She was nominated for an Emmy for her performance as a Scandinavian spinster in the series *I Remember Mama.* We offered Ellen the role of Grandma Walton and she accepted it.

An equally fortunate acceptance came when Edgar Bergen agreed to play Grandpa. Mr. Bergen was a beloved Dane, a quick-witted ventriloquist whose alter ego, Charlie McCarthy, had entertained radio and stage audiences for years.

This was not the first time that Ellen Corby and Edgar Bergen were to perform together. When Ellen was nominated for her portrayal of Trina, the timid old maid in *I Remember Mama,* her suitor was an equally timid undertaker—Edgar Bergen.

More exciting names were signed: Dorothy Stickney and Josephine Hutchinson, both well-known stage actresses, agreed to play the eccentric ladies who made the recipe; William Windom to play Charlie Snead, the "Robin Hood of the Blue Ridge"; Cleavon Little as Hawthorne Dooley, the minister of the local black church. Good friends joined the cast as well: Andrew Duggan as Clay Spencer Sr. and David Huddleston as the county sheriff. Woody Palfrey was proprietor of the local country store.

Just as meaningful to the project as the adult actors were the children who were to play the Spencer brothers and sisters. Casting agent Pam Polifroni searched Hollywood for young actors who answered my father's description of his children as "thoroughbreds." And she found them in a talented crowd of fresh faces: good-looking, redheaded, mischievous, eager, willing, high-spirited youngsters who were to play my brothers and sisters.

Jon Walmsley was born February 6, 1956, in Blackburn, England, and was brought to the United States by his parents while he was still a baby. He graduated from John H. Francis Polytechnic High School and is a gifted musician. I cast my vote for Jon to play the role of Jason Walton the minute I laid eyes on him.

Jon even looked like a Hamner, with his fine crop of hair and abundance of freckles. He was to portray my brother Cliff, which he did with empathy and understanding. Jon had a special gift—his talent for music—and over the years we expanded on that extra talent he brought to the role.

Judy Norton, as an actress, brought the same spirit of independence and strength of character that my sister Marion possessed from the day she was born. Judy was born in Santa Monica, California, January 29, 1958, and after elementary and junior high she enrolled at Grant High School in the San Fernando Valley. It was interesting to see Judy and Marion when they first met. I think they both recognized that they shared so many of the same character traits.

Mary McDonough was to play the "middle child," a role based on my sister Audrey. The middle child is said to be the easygoing child, the patient one who doesn't rock the boat. Audrey was easygoing, but she rocked the boat when she had to! It wasn't easy being the middle child in that pack of brothers and sisters. Mary McDonough played Audrey perfectly. Mary was born May 4, 1961, and with her blue eyes, red hair, and freckles she did not need makeup to have the "Walton" look. She and Audrey became good friends.

Eric Scott was an appealing actor when we auditioned him. His red hair and freckles qualified him immediately as a member of the family, and his ready smile and spirited personality made him perfect casting. Eric probably had the most challenging job of all. The network had grumbled that the cast was too large, and they decreed that the characters of two of my brothers be combined. Eric got the job of playing a composite of my brothers Paul and Bill. He did it very well.

Top, Cleavon Little. *Above,* The Baldwin sisters, portrayed by Dorothy Stickney and Josephine Hutchinson.

Left, Mary McDonough as Erin Walton. *Below,* Ben (Eric Scott) and Jim-Bob (David Harper).

Kami Cotler as Elizabeth feeds Chance the cow.

We cast David Harper in the role of Jim-Bob. The character of Jim-Bob was based on my brother Jim, in life and in the writing of the series an endearing and memorable figure. David was born October 4, 1961, in Abilene, Texas. He came by his acting talents naturally. His father was a TV and movie actor, and his mother was a songwriter.

David played Jim-Bob with just the right amount of innocence in the early episodes. But as time passed and the character grew, it was fun to watch David adjust and grow and mature as he acted the role.

Kami Cotler was to play Elizabeth, based on the character of my sister Nancy, the youngest of the children. She was only six years old when we started work. Kami was a petite person with a charming smile framed by burnished copper-colored hair. She was born in 1965 and celebrates her birthday on June 17. Even at the age of six she had an inquiring mind and an astonishingly adult awareness of the world and the people in it. It is a mark of her ability that she could hold her own against the most experienced scene-stealers, and we were blessed with plenty of those!

Patricia Neal and Earl Hamner at a program honoring *The Waltons* sponsored by the Smithsonian Institution.

The go-ahead to make the film arrived in late summer. If we were to make the film in time for Christmas we had to find snow. It was determined that the only place where we stood any chance at all of getting snow was in the Grand Tetons of Wyoming, where *Spencer's Mountain* had been filmed.

So Fielder Cook, Bob Jacks, and I flew to Jackson Hole, selected locations, and made arrangements to bring in our cast and crew.

Today Jackson Hole is the home of movie stars and rich folks who visit their second homes in their private planes. It was a less sophisticated small town back in those days. The smell of evergreens permeated everything. The air was brisk and clean. There were elk grazing in pastures and fly fishermen casting in brilliantly clear trout streams. And always in one direction the magnificent snow crested the Grand Tetons. It was an invigorating place, and our Los Angeles actors lost no time in getting acquainted and forming relationships that were to last longer than we might have expected.

Among the new arrivals were my wife, Jane, and our children, Scott and Caroline. I always did my best to make it clear to the children where I went when I left home in the morning, what my day was like, and what I did for a living, so on this occasion I arranged for Scott and Caroline to appear in the film as extras. They were pleased about it, but it was a bit challenging for young people raised on sunshine and orange juice to pass as children of the Depression. They did well, good actors both, but I think the expe-

Earl's children, Scott *(above, left)* and Caroline *(above, right),* appeared as extras in *The Homecoming.*

rience proved to them that the life of an actor was one they did not care to pursue.

Fielder had gone to some pains to arrange the filming schedule so that Patricia Neal would not have to go on location. When Pat heard of it she was offended.

"Of course," she insisted, "I will go on location!"

Who said she was not physically ready to film in high wind, deep snow, and wintry weather? In that mighty Wurlitzer organ she calls a voice, she staved off all objections and went with the rest of the cast and crew to Jackson Hole.

The filming went well. In an early scene the script called for snow, but it was early fall and snow at that time of year was rare. And then Fielder worked a miracle. The cameras started rolling. Fielder called, "Action!" The actors started doing their thing. Fielder looked up to heaven and said, "Now, Sir, if You please?"

And snow started to fall.

The actors fell into their roles, the weather stayed favorable, snow fell when Fielder requested it, the sun appeared when sun was needed. Fielder devised one breathtaking scene after another: the Spencer children, all in a row, crossing a snowy field; the Staples ladies in their horse-drawn sleigh traveling down a moonlit country road; Clay-Boy and his grandfather walking through mountainous backcountry to cut down the Christmas tree.

Our exterior filming completed, we returned to California to shoot our interior scenes at the CBS Studio on Radford Avenue in Studio City. Each day at noon we gathered in a small projection room to see the film that had been shot the day before. Interior scenes tend to demand more emotional depth than outdoor action ones. As the days passed, it soon became clear that our young actors were not only highly professional, but each one was a bandit—they stole every scene they were in.

The filming was completed in the late fall and turned over to the editors, Marge and Gene Fowler. They spliced the film together into an "assembly," and then along with Fielder Cook they began the work of editing. Eventually a "director's" cut evolved and finally a "rough" cut, and this was the first time I saw the movie from start to finish. Even in its rough state each of us knew it was a fine piece of work.

One development was of special significance to me. There is a short piece of narration in the beginning of the script. It talks about mountains and families who live in mountains and the significance of this special mountain to the people I wrote about. We auditioned several professional people in Hollywood who specialize in this kind of voice-over work. Nobody sounded quite right. Finally, Fielder Cook said, "What we need is someone who sounds as corny as Earl." He thrust a microphone in front of me. I read the copy and was given the job of narrator! Because of union regulations I had to join SAG and AFTRA, and I was even paid to do work that was totally pleasurable and rewarding. It made me aware of something I had not appreciated before—my voice. I learned that it is "courtly" and "gentle" and "warm" and soothing"! Whatever quality it has, it seems to be distinctive. Often people I meet for the first time will give me a puzzled look and ask, "Why is your voice so familiar?"

The film became even more beautiful once Jerry Goldsmith's score was added. The score is sensitive to every scene it underscores. There are times when the music sings and other times when it subtly underscores the suspense of the long wait, but throughout it is illustrative of the fact that we were incredibly fortunate to have a Jerry Goldsmith score.

The film was aired on CBS on Christmas Eve of 1971. The critics' reviews were uniformly wonderful. The audience share (the percentage of viewers actually watching at the time) was 39, which was stunning. Equally gratifying were the letters from the audience, which began to arrive for the actors, the network, and the production company.

The CEO of CBS at the time was William Paley. Mr. Paley was vacationing in the Bahamas when the film was shown. When he learned of the success of the movie he asked to see it. A copy of the film was delivered to the Bahamas. Paley screened it and sent word back to his executives that he wanted the movie to become the basis for a series.

"We've been taking from the barrel for too long," he said. "It's time we put something back."

Earl records narration for *The Waltons*.

The development of a television series is a precarious thing. It is a long process to begin with, and it must run a gamut of people armed with cudgels labeled "Too Soft," "Too Expensive," "Not Violent Enough," "Not Sexy Enough," "I Hate It!" "Will They Get It in Iowa?" During the birthing process, the infant is at the mercy of studio executives, their wives and children, executives of independent production companies, agents, stars, directors, and members of Congress, not to mention advertisers.

Often what starts out as a golden egg becomes a dead chicken by the time it reaches the airwaves. Sometimes, by a miracle, a project falls into the right hands rather than into those that would kill it. Fortunately, *The Waltons* fell into the hands of caring, creative, and knowledgeable people.

Richard Thomas, Earl Hamner, and Will Geer relaxing on the set.

The machinery of putting together a television series was set in motion. We were way ahead since we had a cast that had already proved they worked well together. Still, network folks need to make their mark on a project or else they feel they have not done their jobs. Consequently they dictated some cast changes. Even though Pat Neal had shown she was the same capable, talented, unique star she had always been, the network was uneasy about her health and suggested the role of the mother be recast.

Michael Learned was a godsend. She is an extraordinarily beautiful woman with talent to match. There was little in her background that would seem to prepare her to portray a woman from the backwoods of Virginia, but Michael proved to be a superb choice. She was the daughter of a diplomat, one of six sisters, and had spent many of her growing-up years in Europe. At sixteen she married actor Peter Donat. The marriage ended in 1972. She divided her time between stage acting and raising her sons. She had a long association with San Francisco's American Conservatory Theater. While appearing in a production of Noel Coward's *Private Lives,* Michael was selected to play the role based on my mother, Olivia Walton.

We were of the opinion that Richard Thomas was our star, but the network insisted we sign an additional star. We sent a copy of the book and a tape of the film to Henry Fonda, who was appearing in a stage play in Chicago. Lee Rich and I flew to Chicago and met with Fonda on one of those impossibly cold and windy Chicago winter days. Even the frosty winter air in the Blue Ridge had not prepared me for the mean winds of January in Chicago. It was a Sunday and we met Fonda in the office of the Leo Burnett advertising agency, where Lee had friends. He had gotten a little grayer than the last time I had seen him, but he was still that same down-to-earth, man of the people, straight shooter I remembered.

Fonda remembered me from our *Spencer's Mountain* days. He had screened the tape of *The Homecoming,* and I still remember his exact words: "This is homespun material," he said, "and I love this kind of thing, but this show belongs to the boy and I'm too old to play second fiddle to a fifteen-year-old kid."

And that settled that.

Ralph Waite was signed to play the father. Ralph took an interesting road on his way to becoming an actor. After earning his B.A.

at Bushnell University, Ralph became a social caseworker in New York's Westchester County. Following that he spent three years at the Yale School of Divinity where he was a practicing Presbyterian minister. He left the ministry to take a job as religious editor at the publishing firm of Harper and Row, and finally he found his true calling—acting. His 1965 role in the play *Hogan's Goat* was to become the true beginning to his lifelong career.

In a speech I once said that actors have rich gifts to give and that Ralph Waite gave me a precious gift in his portrayal of the role inspired by my father, John Walton.

Miraculously, Will Geer became available and took on the role of the grandfather. Will enjoyed the role because he was just being himself. He loved Virginia and he loved Virginians. One of the television reviews once called *The Waltons* "corny." Will remembered the review because he treasured it. I will never forget an occasion when I was being honored at Lovingston, the county seat of Nelson County, Virginia. In the midst of the ceremony there was a commotion at the edge of the football stadium. It turned out to be Will Geer arriving. He had been appearing in a play down in Alabama, and he and a troupe of actors had driven all night to be with me that morning. From some farmer's field down the road he had stolen a bushel of corn, to make the point, as Will said when he presented it to me, that "the country is still under more corn than concrete."

Will didn't play Grandpa. He *was* Grandpa!

We went on the air on September 14, 1972. John McGreevey's story of a little deaf girl abandoned on the Waltons' doorstep was our first show. It was fifty-seventh in the Nielsen ratings, and while the critics' reviews were favorable, most of them predicted that the show would be canceled in short order.

New York Times television critic John J. O'Connor gave the new series a warm and very positive review. It ended by saying: "*The Waltons* deserve an audience. Competing with *Mod Squad* and *Flip Wilson* at the same hour, it won't get one easily. If nothing else, it will be interesting to see if the public has any appetite for good family entertainment."

Life magazine's reviewer Cyclops said, "Confronted with wholesomeness, a critic wants to stab it to death with his 19-cent Bic ballpoint pen. Yet, I liked *The Waltons*. Only a churl would not."

Robert Berkvist in the *New York Times* was more specific. "What does this story of yesterday's people say to us, here, now? Most of us will never know what it's like to live in a sprawling old house with a screen door that slams and cocks that crow in the barnyard. Most of our children won't have run through grassy fields alight with wildflowers. Few of us would give a stranger the time of day, let alone shelter. *The Waltons* reminds us of where we have been and suggests there was value there . . . a time when both young and old had their own dignity. 'It was a poor time,' reflects John-Boy looking back, 'but in it we were richer than we knew.'"

Critic Alan Bunce reviewed the opening show affirmatively, but he reported, "'Insiders' are already calling this entry a probable loser in the all-important ratings game."

Bob Brock of the *Dallas Times Herald* put it this way: "Easily the most creative and brilliantly executed series of this new season is *The Waltons*. It may be one of the most short-lived because of the suicidal slotting by the network." He predicted that *The Waltons* would "receive rave reviews, be embraced by a small, but enthusiastic audience, collect a number of awards and vanish from the air with hardly a ripple."

For a few weeks it appeared that the gloomy prediction of an early cancellation would come to pass. But Lorimar and CBS, encouraged by warm reviews from critics and audience alike, took steps. Merv Adelson recalls the pride we all took in the series and Lorimar's determination to keep the show on the air. A full-page ad was placed in every major newspaper in the country. Its banner read: "This Program Is Too Beautiful to Die!" Lee Rich, the president of the company, wrote to every television critic in the country. In his letter Lee asked for the reviewers' continued support in telling the audience about the series.

Several reviewers responded in their columns. Norman Dresser of the *Toledo Blade* wrote: "I will go out on a limb and state categorically that *The Waltons* is the best dramatic series of the season. It is moving, warm, and beautiful. But I must end on a note of sadness. They say your show hasn't a ghost of a chance (against the competition). Well, maybe they're right, but I'm going to watch your show week after week, and I hope my readers will do so too."

Mary Wood of the *Cincinnati Post* responded with this appeal to her readers: "This is the kind of series so many of you have been begging for, friends. Now that it's here I hope you'll watch it. Need I say that's the only way it will stay on the air.'"

Cynics shook their heads knowingly. What idiot would have programmed a show about a bunch of ignorant hillbillies from backwoods Virginia who lived during the years of the Great Depression in a prime slot like eight o'clock on a Thursday night opposite *The Mod Squad* on ABC and *Flip Wilson* on NBC? The rumor was that CBS would keep the show on the air the few weeks it would take for the "Old Man," as Mr. Paley was called, to come to the conclusion he had been wrong. The least it could do was to give the programmers time to figure out what really ought to go in that time slot.

I think my acting and directing friends will agree that *The Waltons* was a writer's show. In film it all begins with the word, and because of the personal nature of the material I insisted on being in control of the script. It was a heavy responsibility because not only did I have my own scripts to write, I had to meet with other writers to discuss ideas and assign writers to keep freelance scripts coming in. The plot ideas had to be cleared with the network, then each script had to be assigned, typed, printed, and distributed. Often notes from the network or from a cast reading would require a major rewrite. I carried that burden alone for a while until Carol McKeand, who had been in development at Lorimar, accepted the job of script editor. Carol has a fine story sense, a calm approach to the daily calamity of television production, and a unique sense of humor. I was drowning in work until Carol came to help me. She literally saved my life.

Immediately after the first episode there was one special reaction I was anxious to receive. For each Walton character there was a real-life Hamner. The family had loved *The Homecoming,* but what would they think of a character portraying them week by week, often in stories based on their experiences in life or their personalities? My mind was put at ease when I received a letter from my sister Nancy. In it she said, "Thank you for letting us relive some of the happiest days of our lives."

Once my mind was put to rest it was a surprisingly relaxed and pleasurable time for me. Usually with a new series the network will

Michael Learned (Olivia) and Ralph Waite (John) in the Waltons' kitchen.

hover over it and try to "fix" it even before it goes on the air, even before there is anything wrong with it, even before the first episode is aired. With *The Waltons* the assumption was that the series would fail. Consequently there was very little interference. Story editor Carol McKeand, the writers we hired, and I had a choice about the stories we wrote. Most of television is written from the groin. We wrote stories from the heart. We wrote stories we wanted to tell, often stories we never expected to see on television, stories about real people.

And thankfully, the audience found the show! Friends told other friends about it. Mail flowed into the network and into the production office in praise of the show, asking for cast autographs, asking questions about the "real" family the series was based upon, wanting to know more about our actors. Ministers wrote that they found themes for their Sunday sermons in some of the episodes. Other viewers wrote that they moved events scheduled for Thursday nights to another night so they might see first runs of the show. We heard from families who made a habit of watching the show

The cast of *The Waltons:* 1st row: Judy Norton, Eric Scott, Mary McDonough; 2nd row: Jon Walmsley, Ellen Corby, Will Geer, Kami Cotler, David Harper; 3rd row: Ralph Waite, Richard Thomas, Michael Learned.

together and college students gathered in their dorms to share the experience. I remember visiting a friend in the hospital one Thursday evening, and as I made my way down the corridor to her room I passed one open door after another. The TV sets in every room were tuned to the show!

To this day I receive letters from the audience. Most often people thank me for providing the kind of show they can watch with their children. Others will tell me that the series reminded them of their own life experience or else it reminded them of the way they wish their life had been. Sometimes a writer would even tell of an especially intimate personal experience. One of the first such letters I received was from a teenage girl. She had run away from her home in Ohio because of a conflict with her family. She had wandered to Hollywood, become addicted to drugs, and been driven to prostitution to buy food and drugs. One night in a youth shelter she watched one of our episodes. The portrayal of the Walton family made her homesick for her own family. She called home, and her parents pleaded with her to return. She did, and at the time of her letter to me she was back in Ohio. The conflict was still there, but she and her parents were trying to work it out and she was in treatment for drug addiction. I have received other letters of a similar vein over the years. It is an incredibly rewarding experience to learn that you have changed the lives of people you have never met, but whom you have come in contact with through words you have written.

All through September, October, and November, the ratings went up. The rise was not dramatic, but gradual. Point by point. What was important was that the movement continued in an upward direction. We allowed ourselves to hope that at the least, we would not be canceled before the end of the season.

In December 1972 the *New York Times* critic published a column called "The Best of 1972 . . . and the Worst." "First," the article began, "The best:"

> *The Waltons*: As learned treatises were churned out on TV's "new permissiveness," the best new series of the year encompasses a large and poor family in the mountains of Virginia. Set in the Depression years, the weekly series provides

unabashedly sentimental lessons in such old fashioned items as family closeness, respect, pride and responsibility.

Placed by the Columbia Broadcasting System against formidable opposition the series was given little chance for survival in the action-entertainment syndrome of television. It has survived and has been showing surprisingly encouraging progress in the ratings barometers.

We took hope!

That was December of 1972. By the end of the season *The Waltons* was number one in the ratings, and when the Emmys were handed out in May of 1973, Cecil Smith wrote in the *Los Angeles Times,* "*The Waltons,* to nobody's surprise, was voted the best series and won five other awards—actor Richard Thomas, actress Michael Learned, supporting actress Ellen Corby, Marjorie and Gene Fowler for best editing in a drama series, plus the writing award to John McGreevey."

The series would stay on the air for nine full seasons. On some Thursday nights it was seen by as many as fifty million viewers. It won many awards in the years to come. For my own work on the series I received the Christopher Award; I was voted Virginian of the Year by the Virginia Press Association; I received an Honorary Degree from my alma mater, the University of Richmond; and I received the highest honor that can be bestowed in journalism, the George Foster Peabody Award from the University of Georgia.

One of my favorite comments on the series came from President George Bush. At the Republican National Convention in Houston, Texas, August 17, 1992, President Bush said, "Well, let me tell you something; we are going to keep on trying to strengthen the American family, to make American families a lot more like the Waltons and a lot less like the Simpsons."

In the following chapter you will find synopses of each of the episodes as well as the specials that followed after the regular series completed its run. As I was compiling this book I spoke to many of those who took part in the production, and I have included some of their special comments and favorite memories.

Enjoy!

Chapter Five

The Waltons on the Air

❧

Season One (1972–1973)

The Foundling

Air date: 9/14/72; Writer: John McGreevey; Director: Vincent Sherman
Holly, a six-year-old deaf girl, is abandoned on the Waltons' doorstep. They lovingly care for her and teach her sign language, but their attention causes Elizabeth to be jealous. While playing with Holly, Elizabeth accidentally gets locked in a trunk. She is rescued with the help of Holly using sign language.

> *This was the first script I wrote for* The Waltons. *It was my privilege and good fortune to have written twenty episodes of the series. Each was special to me at the time of my involvement. Although I had been working as a television writer for twenty-two years, this was a unique experience. The rumor was that the network felt there would be only the original thirteen shows and that the series was just a sop to placate the reformers in the U.S. Congress who were concerned about the predominance of sex and violence on network television. Consequently there was little if any outside interference. Many other writers and I were able to tell stories close to our hearts—stories for which there had been no outlet.*
>
> JOHN McGREEVEY, WRITER

> *This episode was especially memorable because there was another little girl on the set. We all had to learn sign language, and I still remember my finger alphabet today. I had to spell out "haunted house," which is extremely long when you're only seven. If you watch the scene you can see my lips moving as I struggle to keep the letters straight. Most excitingly, this is the episode where I get locked in a trunk—a major stunt to a little girl as it involved darkness. I*

sat huddled in the corner of the trunk, grasping my doll and they'd close the lid on me. Total darkness. I think I held my breath, waiting for the cameras to start rolling, the director to yell action and the scene to progress until, finally, Ralph tore open the lid of the trunk and rescued me. In between shots, the lid would open and the makeup man would spray me with a water bottle simulating sweat. I have a clear kiddies' sense memory of the lid lifting, the bright lights flooding in and a looming silhouette spritzing my face and hair. I know I felt a great sense of achievement, because the crew, actors, and directors were so proud of me. That sense of being a trouper was a big part of acting to me. I was never sure I was a talented actress, but I was always proud of doing my part.

KAMI COTLER, ACTOR (ELIZABETH WALTON)

When Earl asked me to share my thoughts regarding a favorite from The Waltons, *my remark to him was "Now Earl, that is like asking me to choose between my kids." I shall always remember with fondness the evening of September 14, 1972, as I gathered my family around the TV for an hour of "togetherness." As the Walton theme song began, a feeling of warmth enveloped me and I knew in my heart this was my program. It not only captured my heart but the hearts of my children also.*

Earl Hamner with Carolyn Grinnell at a Fan Club reception.

In the Walton home there was always room for "one" more whether it be a stray animal or a stray person. The home on Walton's Mountain was indeed a home where love permeated the atmosphere, as was evident in this very special episode for me. It was with "hands of love" that a little girl learned to understand and to be understood. Hands of love taught Holly, an abandoned deaf girl, sign language, which resulted in her being reunited with her mother and father. Every time I watch "The Foundling" I want to reach out to those special children. In the fall of 1995 I really learned what it was like to know a special child. Justin, our two-year-old grandson, was diag-

nosed as being autistic. Five years later we once again received
devastating news. He had cancer. As we sat in the holding room at
Brenner's Children's Hospital waiting for his surgery, my heart was
broken. Trapped within his small, fragile body were not only the
pain of cancer but all his emotions too. His countenance was that
of fear and uncertainty as was with Little Holly when she couldn't
understand. As the nurse rolled Justin out of the room for his
surgery and the door closed, I wrapped my arms around my
daughter and we sobbed. Our faith, our love, and family togetherness and our host of friends sustained us.

John-Boy and his family reached out and embraced a child
with special needs. It made a difference. As we continue to watch
The Waltons and glean lessons from the various episodes, may
we reach out to those less fortunate. It will make a difference.
Thank you, John McGreevey, for a heart-warming, uplifting
episode.

CAROLYN GRINNELL, PRESIDENT OF THE
WALTONS INTERNATIONAL FAN CLUB

The Carnival

Air date: 9/21/72; Writer: Nigel McKeand; Director: Arthur Moreton
The children contribute their carnival money to
Esther's new glasses. When the carnival manager
leaves town with their money, four members are
stranded in the Waltons' barn where they repay
the family's generosity with a private performance. The family helps the group to take a train
to Chicago, where they are to perform at the
World's Fair.

Billy Barty appeared
in "The Carnival."

*I remember my trepidation when I first came to
meet the producers of* The Waltons. *Seemingly
unfazed by my lack of writing experience, they
cheerfully handed me a list of story ideas. I
chose one about the performers of a small tour-
ing carnival who get stranded on the mountain
after the manager has run off with the proceeds. Back home I stared in panic at my typewriter. What had I gotten myself into? I'd never*

written for television before and I'd never been anywhere near Virginia; in fact I had grown up in England. Fortunately, I had spent much of my childhood living near a small village in Scotland with the unlikely name of Auchtermunchty. Was a small village in Scotland so very different from Walton's Mountain? I convinced myself it wasn't. And the problems and the uncertainties that John-Boy was facing growing up were ones with which I could easily identify—as were the lives of the entire Walton family. Slowly, my panic receded, my head cleared, and I saw a small monkey wearing a hat and a velvet vest tapping on the window of Jason and Jim-Bob's bedroom window. I began to type; the pages became a script and the script finally became "The Carnival."

NIGEL MCKEAND, WRITER

This was one of my favorite episodes because it brought all kinds of interesting and exotic people onto the mountain and we found out that they were not all that different from us. One of the carnival people was played by Billy Barty, and I can remember what a nice man he was and what a pleasure it was to meet someone whose work I had seen on television.

MARY MCDONOUGH, ACTOR (ERIN WALTON)

The Calf

Air date: 9/28/72; Writer: Jim Byrnes; Director: Harry Harris
The family cow, Chance, gives birth to a male calf, and John announces that it must be sold to make truck repairs. The bull is sold to a local farmer, Mr. Anderson, but Jim-Bob and Elizabeth hide the calf to save it from slaughter. John finally relents and the family keeps the calf.

This was the first episode I directed. A friend, a TV executive, asked what I was doing and I said I was working on a series about a poor family in the backwoods of Virginia during the Great Depression. He said, "You've got to be kidding. Who would watch that?" "It's going to be a hit," I said. He said, "I'll bet you fifty cents it's canceled in two weeks." I ran into the man about ten years later. He looked at me and smiled and said, "I think I owe you fifty cents."

HARRY HARRIS, DIRECTOR

I enjoy watching each and every episode, and I still get something from them each time I watch. It's so hard to pick out a favorite, but I am partial to the first season. Everyone was sort of growing into their characters, and I enjoy watching them evolve into the older characters as time goes by. After all, I'm watching my brothers and sisters grow up! Plus it's the beginning of the season and I get to start them all over again. Elizabeth and Jim-Bob are so precious in those earlier episodes. I just want to gather them up in my arms and hug them. I love the way Daddy calls her Baby and you will often see her cuddled up in his lap. In "The Calf" she and Jim-Bob cautiously walk over to Daddy as they are about to receive their scolding. I adore their innocence at that moment.

Sharon Holmes, Fan—Chico, California

There is a scene in this episode where all the kids run into the barn to greet the new arrival—Chance's calf. There was some discussion on the set as to whether real farm kids would get all that excited abut the birth of another farm animal. It was decided after some discussion that for the sake of the plot we should definitely be as excited as possible. For me, this proved much more difficult than you might imagine. The day before, I had been to Malibu beach with Judy Norton and Eric Scott. We were out in the sun all day. Judy and Eric, who in spite of his red hair is quite tolerant of the sun, got fabulous tans. I, on the other hand, was burnt to a crisp. As we shot the calf scene, I was in severe pain. I felt like a smile would crack my face and kneeling down to greet Chance's baby was excruciating. Every time I see this scene, I notice Jason running a little slower than the other kids, trying not to grimace as he gingerly lowers himself to the ground to view the new arrival.

Jon Walmsley, Actor (Jason Walton)

The Hunt

Air date: 10/5/72; Writer: John McGreevey; Director: Robert Butler
John-Boy reluctantly goes on his first hunt because he abhors the taking of an animal's life. During the hunt he proves himself not a coward by saving John's life during a bear attack. Mary Ellen can't decide which to buy: a baseball mitt or a dress.

Left, Irene Porter, president of the Walton's Friendship Society, and Earl Hamner. *Below,* Will Geer (Zeb Walton) and Mary Jackson (Miss Emily Baldwin) enjoy fishing.

I remember that "The Hunt" was the first show we filmed, although it was not the first to go on the air. I recall my shock and anxiety to be told that on my first Walton episode I was going to have to wrestle a bear. When I read the script I kind of skipped over the part about bear wrestling and then I got to the set and there was the bear and he was huge! I was about to run off then and there when I was told that the man who trained the bear would actually wrestle with me. He would be dressed in a bear suit and the scene would be shot in such a way that it would appear that I was actually wrestling a bear. I'm glad now I didn't run off because it was the beginning of a lifetime of memories from those extraordinary years we all spent together.

RALPH WAITE, ACTOR (JOHN WALTON)

The Typewriter

Air date: 10/12/72; Writer: Theodore Apstein; Director: Philip Leacock
John-Boy receives a manuscript back from a publisher saying that they require all submissions to be typed. He borrows an antique typewriter from the Baldwin sisters, but Mary Ellen mistakenly sells it to a junk dealer. Through her persistence she gets it back for her brother. Though the submission is rejected, the publisher asks John-Boy to submit other samples of his work.

I especially enjoyed this story of Mary Ellen's accidentally selling to a junkman a typewriter that John-Boy had borrowed from the Baldwin ladies. To be honest it never happened in real life, but who is to say that a story isn't real if it is only invented by a writer? There was a junkman who came around when we were children, and he would buy up scrap iron and aluminum for a few pennies. Earl took a lot of liberties with the facts of our lives, but we always forgave him. I guess it's called "poetic license." Whatever it's called, it provided some good stories and good clean entertainment to millions of people.

MARION HAMNER HAWKES, MODEL FOR MARY ELLEN

John-Boy's frustrated yell of "How am I ever going to grow to be a man in this house!?" captured my attention and eventually led me to having access to TV producers and actors and fellowship with wonderful people all over Britain. As the '70s passed and the characterization of the characters was constant, my admiration grew for this "boy" and the series. It was only meant to be entertainment, but life's lessons are all there for any viewer who takes the time to really watch and absorb each episode.

IRENE PORTER, PRESIDENT,
WALTONS FRIENDSHIP SOCIETY,
SOMERSET, ENGLAND

I loved playing Miss Emily Baldwin. Earl Hamner told me that there really were two ladies in his hometown who made the recipe, but they were mother and daughter rather than sisters, and they served it in a tin dipper rather than the elegant silver goblets we used on the show. I sometimes used to think that Miss Emily's sweetheart who kissed her in October "in a shower of golden leaves" was mostly a product of her imagination. Later I discovered that he was very real to the audience. I will never forget boarding a crowded Madison Avenue bus and a gentleman getting up and offering me his seat and saying, "And how is Ashley Longworth?"

MARY JACKSON, ACTOR (EMILY BALDWIN)

When John-Boy learns that the typewriter is missing he has a classic scene and he plays it to the hilt. Helen Kleeb once told me that the Waltons are the meat and potatoes of the series, but that the Baldwin ladies are the dessert!

DUANE SHELL, FAN—LOS ANGELES, CALIFORNIA

Helen Kleeb, who played Miss Mamie Baldwin, was in ill health as this book was being prepared so I did not disturb her. But I worked with Helen for many years and I know she would want me to say she loved the character of Miss Mamie and enjoyed playing her. The reality is that the Baldwin ladies might have come off as "giddy" or "silly" except for the performances of Mary and Helen. Both ladies are such fine actors that they knew how to give their characters charm and dignity as well as a generous helping of something that both Mary and Helen possess in such abundance—elegance and gentility.

EARL HAMNER, CREATOR AND EXECUTIVE PRODUCER

The Star

Air date: 10/19/72; Writer: John McGreevey; Director: Alf Kjellin
When a meteorite falls on the Baldwins' recipe room, Zeb believes
it is an omen of his death and he takes to bed. Their cousin
Polonius, a con man, hoaxes the Baldwin sisters until Zeb and
John step in. The family proudly displays a scholastic medal won
by Ben at school.

> *Will Geer, the incomparable actor who became Grandpa Zeb
> Walton, brought such energy and humor to the show. It was a par-
> ticular joy to write his scenes. Will and I discovered that we were
> both displaced Hoosiers, which gave us an even closer bond. In
> "The Star" we tried to give Will an opportunity to show the darker
> side of Grandpa. He gives a tour de force performance.*
>
> JOHN MCGREEVEY, WRITER

> *This was the first episode in which I had the subplot. It told about
> Ben's winning the spelling bee and I got sooooo excited, I felt I had
> actually won the prize!*
>
> ERIC SCOTT, ACTOR (BEN WALTON)

The Sinner

Air date: 10/26/72; Writer: John Furia Jr.; Director: Philip Leacock
The new preacher, Matthew Fordwick, has a rocky start on
Walton's Mountain. He upsets John with his strict and forceful
preaching that is disturbing to the children. While visiting the
Baldwin sisters, who are distant relatives, he innocently samples
"the recipe." When he returns home he is observed drunk, but
John helps him to be accepted by the congregation and the town.

> *One of the things I enjoyed about writing for* The Waltons *was its
> unabashed willingness to deal with goodness in people. In "The
> Sinner" I wanted to explore how we often see no deeper than the
> surface in each other. The leading man of the story is a young
> preacher filled with zeal and pride. When he falls from grace, the
> congregation of "good" people shames him. All except for that
> notorious sinner, the hero of the story, John Walton, who is on inti-
> mate terms with human frailty and has the courage and grace to*

John Ritter played the Reverend Matthew Fordwick.

stand up for the decent and humbled young man who succumbed to it.

JOHN FURIA, WRITER

This episode marked the appearance of one of my favorite Walton characters, John Ritter as the Reverend Matthew Fordwick. It was obvious that John was destined for comedic stardom. He kept us laughing constantly. John and Richard Thomas had something of a contest going—to see who could "gross out" the other, preferably while the victim was doing his close-up. Their gorilla act was a standout. They would crouch low to the ground, swing their arms like apes, and emit guttural monkey sounds. A far cry from two actors who not long ago had had a hit on the London stage!

JON WALMSLEY,
ACTOR (JASON WALTON)

A vivid memory of working on The Waltons *was on an episode in which we filmed outdoors on the Warner Brothers lot in a tree-filled area near a lake. It was at a picnic with races and games. Richard Thomas and John Ritter and I were in a series of scenes*

*together that day. Richard and John were great friends—in life as
well as in this episode—and they made each other laugh; oh, how
they made each other laugh. And they both made me laugh. In
between takes it was like being with two great master clowns—
their competing pratfalls, their regular jokes, and their gross-out
jokes. They filled in with each other's punch lines. It would accel-
erate until it was time to do a take and we would become sober.
This respite gave them time to be inspired and start all over again,
even funnier.*

MARICLARE COSTELLO, ACTOR (ROSEMARY HUNTER FORDWICK)

The Boy from the CCC

Air date: 11/02/72; Writer: William Welch; Director: Harry Harris
Gino, a boy from a nearby CCC Camp, is found on the mountain
with an injured ankle. The Waltons take him in, but he has a hard
time accepting the family's kindness. He steals from the family, and
John threatens to turn him in to the sheriff. Elizabeth's pet raccoon
dies.

*Sometimes when you act with someone on a series, you work
together in an episode and then you never see that person again.
When we filmed this episode I had a crush on Michael Rupert,
who played the boy from the CCC. Years later I was with a bunch
of actors in New York and we went backstage to see Michael, who
was starring in Pippin. Years had passed but my heart still
skipped a beat.*

MARY MCDONOUGH, ACTOR (ERIN WALTON)

*In this episode Elizabeth has a pet raccoon named Pete. Pete was
just the beginning of Elizabeth's sick pets, most of which perished
for plot purposes. In the end Pete dies and we hold a funeral service for him. The whole family stood around the grave in the rain.
It was my first filmed rain sequence and the sprinklers atop tall
towers were very impressive. It took hours to film the scene and
we were all drenched to the skin. As the grave filled with water,
the little makeshift casket began to float and we ended up snigger-
ing at jokes about Pete floating away to raccoon heaven.*

KAMI COTLER, ACTOR (ELIZABETH WALTON)

The Ceremony

Air date: 11/09/72; Writer: Nigel McKeand; Director: Vincent Sherman

Professor Mann and his family come to Walton's Mountain to escape Nazi Germany. Their thirteen-year-old son wants to have his bar mitzvah. He loses respect for his father, who he believes does not wish to maintain his religious beliefs and practices. Grandpa Zeb solves the crisis by talking to the father, and the Waltons host the ceremony in their home.

Will Geer's daughter, Ellen, who appeared in several episodes.

I am back in the memories vault with one of the best working experiences I've had and that was with The Waltons *and my pop. We'd played together quite often in the theater, but this was the first time together on television. Living with Pop always brought the larger picture of life into every experience. Playing the mother of a Jewish refugee family in "The Ceremony" hiding during World War II with the comforting of Grandpa Walton, who in real life was my father, gives me forever an exceptional memory. The Walton family was Pop's "other" family and as it was such a good one, it was very easy for the Geer family to share our pop. After Hollywood had turned its back on him during the Blacklist of the McCarthy era, the series presented him back to Hollywood and his country as he truly was: one of the truest Americans, and loved and respected for all his views. My love always,*

ELLEN GEER, ACTOR

There were no Jewish families on Walton's Mountain until the family came in this episode, so the children had no knowledge of Jewish people. We children were discussing the newcomers, and being that I am of Jewish heritage it seemed ironic that I got the line of dialogue "What is a Jew?"

ERIC SCOTT, ACTOR (BEN WALTON)

The Legend

Air date: 11/16/72; Writer: John McGreevey; Director: Lee Philips
John's WWI army buddy, Tip Harrison, comes for a visit and is obviously living in the past. He attempts to cover his lack of success with WWI stories and childish banter. He accidentally starts a fire and, while hunting, accidentally shoots the family dog, Reckless. He eventually confesses to John and John-Boy, and Reckless is rescued.

John McGreevey.

> *As I recall, we wanted an episode that would focus on John Walton. My father was a World War I veteran—as was John. When I was growing up—not on Walton's Mountain but in Indiana—my father's memories of his World War I buddies were very vivid. The particular character in "The Legend" came to be a re-creation of one of those wartime trench-mates.*

> JOHN MCGREEVEY, WRITER

The Literary Man

Air date: 11/30/72; Writer: Colley Kibber; Director: Philip Leacock
When John-Boy's truck breaks down he meets author A. J. Covington. John-Boy and A. J. hit it off and talk all day about writing instead of cutting timber, thus jeopardizing a contract badly needed by the family. Jim-Bob has emergency surgery for appendicitis. The surgery is unexpectedly paid for by A. J., who uses the money he planned to use to buy a house.

> *When the script was sent to me, I was surprised and flattered. After all, I had been known for playing heavies and hard-boiled characters. Now they were asking me to play this gentle, learned man, A. J. Covington. I accepted the job immediately. Philip Leacock was the director, and when we began to shoot, it was obvious that there was a great love among the cast. They all welcomed me into their family with love and understanding. It was a*

great episode. We all loved working on it. Even the cameraman, Russ Metty, who seldom moved from it, got out of his chair on occasion to see some of the beautiful shots. I loved doing the show. I am as proud of that work as any I have done in my long career. I especially loved doing the character of A. J. He was in reality a fraud, but one you loved.

DAVID HUDDLESTON, ACTOR (A. J. COVINGTON)

I had always dreamed of being a writer, so I became one. Just like young John Walton Jr., I knew that writers were dreamers of the grand and the glorious, taking simple language and saturating it with breath and soul.

As a correspondent for a small-town newspaper, I often feel stifled and jaded by journalism. When I need a light on the horizon, I seek the company of John-Boy and A. J. Covington in "The Literary Man." This episode grounds me, brings me back to my center. It reminds me of all the reasons I love to write. And when the piece I am working on seems too difficult, or too plain and mundane, I remember that it doesn't have to be that one barn-burner of an article I was born to write. It is enough that it is a story, any story.

I am proud of the literary craft. At times it takes courage and conviction to carry on. When I get tossed about on the sea of deadlines and dead ends, of adjective-chopping and writer's block, I have found a true and treasured friend in this episode. When I am lost, it lends me wings with which to fly myself home.

JAMIE MOREWOOD ANDERSON, FAN—
CEDAR CREST, NEW MEXICO

The Dust Bowl Cousins

Air date: 12/07/72; Writer: Paul Savage; Director: Robert Butler
The Denby family, Ham, Cora, and Job, distant cousins, arrive on the mountain and upset everyone's life by stealing from Ike and fighting with Mary Ellen and John-Boy. Ham plans to get some of the Walton land that he accuses the family of stealing from Cora. Zeb sets him straight and they move on at Cora's insistence.

"If you want to taste the cherries, you have to climb the tree." This line from "The Dust Bowl Cousins" was the spine of the story that

to me epitomized the work ethic of the Walton family. While coping with ongoing Depression-era trials and tribulations, they selflessly helped—physically and emotionlessly—ones in more dire straits.

PAUL SAVAGE, WRITER

Bob Jacks, the producer, called me. I was on location in June Lake, California, doing a picture with Clint Eastwood called High Plains Drifter. "Can you get free a couple of days next week?" said Bob. "I'm doing a series taken from The Homecoming, the Christmas special. "Count me in," I said. "I saw it and I loved it. That was my time. I knew those people." I went to Clint and asked him if I could get loose for a couple of days. He checked and they figured they could let me go. I came down to Warner Brothers Studio and found out that Ralph Waite, whom I had just done Cool Hand Luke with, was starring as Papa Walton. I said, "Ralph, this is a beautiful show." He said, "Yeah, it is, but we're not going to be here more than ten minutes. We are up against Flip Wilson and Mod Squad. We'll be lucky if we last a year." We still get a laugh about that.

BOB DONNER, ACTOR (YANCY TUCKER)

A family once stayed with the Waltons for a few days, a cousin and her husband and a son sadly less decent and honorable than their hosts, whom they began to taint and darken and sour, and it was painful to watch happening. Of course the family had to be asked to move on, and they did. And the experience of that story for us all was strong and deep and rich. A great lesson and a clear example of what we all know and could share as what's true. As was so often the case with the show—this was simply warming terrific story stuff.

BOB BUTLER, DIRECTOR

The Reunion

Air date: 12/14/72; Writer: Earl Hamner; Director: Jack Shea
Cousin Homer Lee Baldwin comes for a visit and tries to scam the ladies of their "recipe." John-Boy buys a used washing machine for his mother. The Baldwins plan for a big family reunion but no one comes. The entire Walton family attends the party instead.

The Minstrel

Air date: 12/21/72; Writer: John Furia Jr.; Director: Philip Leacock
Mary Ellen feels trapped in her surroundings and becomes
attracted to Jamie, a traveling troubadour. John has contracted
with a nearby orchard to pick fruit. The entire family works hard
except Mary Ellen, who wants to run away with Jamie. John-Boy
breaks his wrist and the family is hard put to finish their apple-
picking contract. They do finish on time and the family chips in to
send Mary Ellen to Washington, D.C., for an adventure.

The Actress

Air date: 1/04/73; Writer: William Best; Director: Vincent Sherman
The famous actress Alvira Drummond finds herself stranded on
Walton's Mountain with car trouble. Her driver absconds with her
money. The Waltons take her in and all the family, except
Grandma, are fascinated by her "Big City" ways. John-Boy refers to
her as "a New York Hurricane." Alvira puts on a performance in
Ike's store to earn money to pay her fare to New York City.

The Fire

Air date: 1/11/73; Writer: Earl Hamner; Director: Harry Harris
Lutie Bascomb, Lois May's father, objects to Miss Hunter teaching
the theory of evolution to her students. Since his wife left him he
does not permit Lois May to talk to boys. During a drunken rage
he vandalizes and burns down the school and is killed in the fire.
Lois May is reunited with her mother

*Sometimes the writers would come up with my opening and clos-
ing narration, but often it would not be just exactly the way I
wanted to say it and I would have to write it myself. Here is one
piece of a closing narration I always liked because it captured to
my satisfaction that feeling back home when we all said
"Goodnight."*

*The house is hushed now, the hour is late. The night is
still except for a whippoorwill that calls from the
crabapple tree. From the kitchen I hear the voices of
my mother and father as they speak quiet private
things to each other. Night flows through the house like*

*a quiet river. Soon the sleep of my mother and my
father and of my brothers and sisters will join the flow
of that quiet river and we will dream our separate
dreams.*

EARL HAMNER, CREATOR AND EXECUTIVE PRODUCER

The Love Story

Air date: 1/18/73; Writer: Earl Hamner; Director: Lee Philips
John-Boy discovers love in the person of Jenny Pendleton. While
her father and new stepmother are on their honeymoon, Jenny
runs away to the family home on Walton's Mountain. Jenny's father
and stepmother arrive looking for her and decide to open the family home. John-Boy takes Jenny to see the remains of Rome
Walton's cabin on top of the mountain. Later, her father is killed in
an auto accident and Jenny returns to Richmond with her stepmother. John-Boy suffers his first lost love.

> *This was such a very innocent love story. We did not need graphic
> sexual scenes to know how deeply in love this young couple is. My
> heart broke for John-Boy when Jenny had to leave. I remember
> seeing it for the first run of the series and I've never forgotten it. It
> still brings tears to my eyes when I watch it.*
>
> JENNI WISEMANN, FAN—MICHIGAN CITY, INDIANA

The Courtship

Air date: 1/25/73; Writer: Jeb Rosebrook; Director: Harry Harris
Olivia's uncle Cody Nelson, laid off from his job at a bank in
Cincinnati, comes to visit the Waltons. He is very conservative and
set in his ways but surprisingly finds romance with Cordelia
Hunnicut, who has been divorced four times. They marry and
return to Cincinnati.

> *Writing scripts for* The Waltons *was, for me, like going back to
> my home in Carter's Bridge, Virginia. Someone asked me where
> this story of a lifelong bachelor and an oft-married spendthrift
> zesty lady came from. Willie Nelson once told Merle Haggard how
> inspiration for stories or songs came about: "We're not in charge,"
> he said.*
>
> JEB ROSEBROOK, WRITER

The Gypsies

Harry Harris.

Air date: 2/01/73; Writer: Paul Savage; Director: Harry Harris
A stranded Gypsy family refuses to accept help from the Waltons until Grandma saves the baby's life. Their dog, accused of killing chickens, is found to have killed a fox, the real culprit.

Most of the time things went smoothly on the set, but on this episode something spooked the Gypsies' horse. It bolted right through the brick entryway to the Baldwin house and knocked the whole thing down. Thankfully the ladies were enjoying the recipe and weren't too upset.

HARRY HARRIS, DIRECTOR

The Deed

Air date: 2/08/73; Writer: James Menzies; Director: Vincent Sherman
Grandpa and John-Boy come across a survey team plotting a new road on Walton's Mountain. They learn that the Waltons never officially registered the deed to Walton's Mountain. In order to help pay the legal fees, Mary Ellen sells an antique teapot and John-Boy leaves home for a job in the city. While there, he gets mugged but earns a reward, and the family registers the deed.

The Scholar

Air date: 2/22/73; Writer: John McGreevey; Director: Lee Philips
A neighbor, Verdie Grant, asks John-Boy to teach her to read and write so that she will not embarrass her daughter at graduation. Since he is already helping Elizabeth, he agrees to Verdie's request. She asks John-Boy to keep their arrangement private, but Elizabeth sees them and tells Miss Hunter, the teacher. Verdie accuses John-Boy of betrayal but later learns the truth. John McGreevey won an Emmy for this episode.

This was a story I had long wanted to tell. This would be an adult who can't read or write and finds himself/herself in a situation where the secret will be an excruciating embarrassment. So John-Boy teaches this person to read and write. This is a woman, a mother, who dreads embarrassing a daughter about to graduate from college up north. I remember that story conference with Earl and story editor Carol McKeand. As we talked I had a daring thought: Suppose the woman is black. This is Virginia after all. And so, the first African-American character joined the Waltons' extended family—and stayed. Lynn Hamilton became Verdie Grant, and we have remained close friends.

JOHN MCGREEVEY, WRITER

This was my favorite episode for several reasons. In it my character, Verdie Grant, was introduced in John McGreevey's beautifully crafted, poignant, and entertaining script, for which he justly won an Emmy! Verdie could neither read nor write and spent most of her time trying to hide that fact. When the time came when she could no longer hide, John-Boy agreed to tutor her. A whole new world opened up and her life began anew. This story inspired many people, adults and young dropouts, to continue their education, that it's never too late to learn, that one is never too old to learn, and that is the best gift you can give yourself.

Lynn Hamilton and Will Geer, as Verdie Grant Foster and Zeb Walton.

LYNN HAMILTON, ACTOR
(VERDIE GRANT FOSTER)

In the role of Verdie Grant we were fortunate to be able to cast Miss Lynn Hamilton. Fans will remember Lynn's memorable appearances as a regular on Sanford and Son *as well as the distinguished miniseries* Roots, *in which she costarred. She presently makes her home in Los Angeles and is married to the poet Frank Jenkins. When she is not busy acting Lynn loves to travel, and under President Kennedy's Cultural Exchange Program she toured Europe, Central America, and South America. Lynn was scheduled to appear in only one*

Lynn Hamilton.

episode of the series, but her presence was so warm and her personality so engaging we persuaded her to become a permanent member of the cast and to remain on the series for the run of the show.

EARL HAMNER, CREATOR AND EXECUTIVE PRODUCER

I think this is one of the most important episodes of the whole series. It helped people see that literacy is not an incurable condition. Verdie learned to read and write and this encouraged folks in the audience, who had the same problem, that they too could learn. It also introduced us to Verdie Grant Foster, who is one of my favorite characters on the show. I now have a wonderful friendship with Lynn Hamilton, all because of my love for The Waltons.

JENNI WISEMANN, FAN—MICHIGAN CITY, INDIANA

The Bicycle

Air date: 3/01/73; Writer: Nigel McKeand; Director: Alf Kjellin
John-Boy agrees to help blacksmith Curtis Norton write letters to Ann Harris, his fiancée. When Ann arrives, Curtis is much different from what she expected. Olivia searches for fulfillment and buys a used bicycle from Ike's store. She comes to realize that her true calling is to be with the family.

The Townie

Air date: 3/08/73; Writer: Richard Fielder; Director: Jack Shea
After going on a date with John-Boy, Sarah Simmonds sees him as a way to escape her boring lifestyle with her domineering mother. John-Boy gently rejects her plans and she decides to elope with a townie named Theodore Claypool. John-Boy goes after them and finds their car overturned on the side of the road. Jim-Bob finds a duck egg and learns from Grandpa how to hatch it. He names the duck "Jim-Bob Junior."

This episode was notable for the casting of the two leading guest actors. The role of Sarah Simmonds was played by Academy

Award–winning actress Sissy Spacek. Sissy lives with her husband and children on a farm in Virginia not far from the real Walton's Mountain.

The role of "The Townie" was played by Nicholas Hammond, who was best known for his work as a child actor when he played Friedrich von Trapp in The Sound of Music. *Nicholas was born in Washington, D.C., and is still an actor. While working on a film in Australia he fell in love with that country and today makes his home in Sydney.*

EARL HAMNER, CREATOR AND EXECUTIVE PRODUCER

The Easter Story

Air date: 4/19/73 (two-hour episode); Teleplay: John McGreevey; Story: Earl Hamner; Director: Philip Leacock

Coming home from church, Olivia collapses and has to be helped into the house. Dr. Vance determines she is suffering from polio and he prescribes the traditional treatment, but Olivia does not get better. John-Boy visits the University of Virginia and talks with a doctor there, who informs him of a new treatment practiced by Sister Kenny in Australia. The doctor visits Olivia and brings more information about the new technique. Spurred on by John-Boy's enthusiasm, the family successfully tries the new method. Meanwhile, Jason wins first prize in an amateur contest with his song "The Ironing Board Blues."

This was the first two-hour show for the series. Olivia is stricken with polio. I was given the assignment. What a challenge! Could we sustain our audience's interest over this doubled time period? Could we find ways to keep all our running characters involved? By this time (spring 1973) the cast, the writers, and the directors had gotten to know one another. I was delighted to have the challenge of two hours. (This was, in a way, a turning point in my career. After The Waltons *I worked only on two-hour movies for television and miniseries.) We didn't rely on our memories for this script. We researched polio and what treatments were available in the thirties. Sister Kenny's approach plays an important role in our treatment. The dual threat of Olivia's threatened loss of her physical strength and John-Boy's threatened loss of his spiritual*

The Register

MONDAY EDITION
LATE NEWS · SPORTS

METROPOLITAN ORANGE COUNTY'S   WATCHFUL NEWSPAPER
ORANGE COUNTY, CALIFORNIA   MONDAY MORNING, MAY 21, 1973   Daily 10¢—Sunday 25¢   68th Year—Number 175

★★★ Four Sections...82 Pages

WALTONS SWEEP EMMY AWARDS

beliefs brought a memorable response from our audience. We were number one that week!

JOHN MCGREEVEY, WRITER

I wrote "The Ironing Board Blues" for Grandma in this episode, and Jason won a guitar performing at a talent show, which he later re-created for the family. Ellen and I sort of looked at "The Ironing Board Blues" as "our song" after that. She was always tremendously supportive of my musical career, and used to invite me to escort her to the Emmys, People's Choice Awards, and such ceremonies.

JON WALMSLEY, ACTOR (JASON WALTON)

When I think of "The Easter Story," it touches my heart as emotions of sadness and joy are intertwined. Once again the strength and love the Walton family felt for one another are evident. Even though Olivia was confined to her bed with polio, her desire to reach out to those she loved burned deep within her soul.

It was through her love and devotion to her child that, even in a dream, a mother heard her child calling in distress. My heart sings with joy as I remember that moment when Olivia took steps to answer Elizabeth's call! In answering this call, Olivia triumphed over what the doctors said was hopeless. With love and support from her family she learned to walk again. As family and friends *gathered facing into the glorious rays of that Easter morning sun, it was indeed a special sunrise service for Olivia.*

As a young mother at the tender age of thirty-four years old, little did I realize the impact Olivia Walton would have on my life. I wanted so much to be like her. In my heart, I felt that she was worthy of emulating. Her love for her husband, her children, and her neighbors was a living lesson in love. Her unwavering faith in God was an example for all to follow. In the fall of 1992, I had the privilege of meeting Michael Learned. Over the years she became my friend, and when she was our guest speaker at our reunion luncheon in October 2000, she paid me a compliment that will be etched in my heart forever. She looked across the banquet room and so lovingly said, "Carolyn and Harold are our John and Olivia."

CAROLYN GRINNELL, PRESIDENT OF THE
WALTON'S INTERNATIONAL FAN CLUB

Season Two (1973–1974)

The Journey

Air date: 9/13/73; Writer: Nigel McKeand; Director: Harry Harris

Neighbor Maggie McKenzie suffers from a weak heart and convinces John-Boy to take her to see the ocean on her wedding anniversary. In so doing, he is unable to take Marcia Woolery to an important school dance. Meanwhile, Grandpa helps the children save an injured seagull. Earl Hamner makes his only appearance in the series as Maggie's husband, seen dancing with her in a dream sequence.

This was a beautifully written episode with a cast to match. I was nominated for an Emmy and a Director's Guild Award for this one. Linda Watkins, who had been a big movie actress, played the old lady who wants to observe her wedding anniversary at Virginia Beach. Linda did a fine acting job, but I can't say the same for the gentleman who played her deceased husband. If you look closely behind the handlebar mustache and the gray hair you'll see our producer, Earl Hamner, of all people. Earl claims the experience was so traumatic he never acted again!

HARRY HARRIS, DIRECTOR

Earl Hamner appearing in "The Journey."

John-Boy's compassion for Maggie McKenzie takes them both on an unforgettable journey. It really is a lovely episode but does not let itself become too sentimental either. I love the characterization of Maggie. And it was good to see Earl Hamner in the role of Maggie's husband, which I understand was his first and last acting job.

NED FARNSWORTH, FAN—LIBENZELL MISSION, ECUADOR, SOUTH AMERICA

The Odyssey

Air date: 9/20/73; Writer: Joanna Lee; Director: Jack Shea

John-Boy, desiring privacy from the family, heads up the mountain and finds a sick and pregnant girl. He visits with Granny Ketchum and she gives him some herbs for the pregnant girl. Upon his return to the cabin, he helps deliver the baby. Meanwhile, Jim-Bob wins a prize for his tomato preserves in a school competition. Granny Ketchum dies and bequeaths the mule Blue to John-Boy.

The Separation

Air date: 9/27/73; Teleplay: Richard Carr; Story: Ellen Corby; Director: Philip Leacock

When the Waltons are unable to pay their electric bill, Grandpa sets out to raise some money but tells no one about his plans. Grandma becomes angry and Grandpa moves out. The bill is paid and the angry grandparents make up at a barn dance, where they dance to their favorite tune, "My Wild Irish Rose."

This episode illustrates the importance of the family unit, which through adversity can be made stronger by recognizing family values. This story was told against a far distant time, but I feel it is a very strong indication of where society would like us to go today.

STEPHEN SPEAR, FAN—CAERPHILLY, ENGLAND

The Theft

Air date: 10/04/73; Writer: Robert Malcom Young; Director: Harry Harris

Some antique silver disappears from the Claybourne home while

John is making repairs. Mrs. Claybourne accuses John but he insists that he is innocent. He pawns his wedding ring to buy much-needed tires, and he refuses to tell anyone where the money came from. The truth comes out when Stuart Lee Claybourne admits to selling the silver to raise money for his family.

> One episode that really stands out in my mind is this one. John is accused of stealing from the Claybournes when it was really a member of the family who took the missing items to sell because his family was out of money. John did not tell anyone he did not steal the silver goblets. He knew he didn't take them. He knew anyone who really knew him would also know he would never take anything that didn't belong to him. He saw no reason to defend himself.
>
> JENNI WISEMANN, FAN—MICHIGAN CITY, INDIANA

The Roots

Air date: 10/11/73; Writer: Sheldon Stark; Director: Philip Leacock
The characters of Harley Foster and his son Jodie are introduced in this episode. Verdie Grant takes a strong liking to Harley and eventually persuades him, with John-Boy's help, to stay on Walton's Mountain, thus establishing a romantic relationship.

> The character of Harley Foster was introduced in this episode. Harley was to become a permanent resident of Walton's Mountain and eventually married Verdie Foster. Harley was played by Hal Williams, who is remembered for his starring role in the television series 227. He is a native of Columbus, Ohio, and attended Ohio State University as well as the Columbia School of Art and Design. His big break came in the series Sanford and Son, in which he had the recurring role of Smitty the cop. His many movie credits include Private Benjamin and Hard Core. Today he makes his home in Hawaii.
>
> EARL HAMNER, CREATOR AND EXECUTIVE PRODUCER

The Chicken Thief

Air date: 10/18/73; Writer: Richard Carr; Director: Ralph Senensky
By chance, John-Boy sees Yancy Tucker stealing chickens and must decide whether to turn him in to the sheriff. Yancy has been help-

ing poor friends, but he is arrested and charged with shooting the chickens' owner in the leg. All is resolved when the owner admits to John that he fell and shot himself. Ben wins a poetry contest in *Liberty* magazine and is concerned about John-Boy's reaction.

> *This was the first episode I directed. When I read the script I realized that in the first act John-Boy declares he is going to be writing biographies of local people. But nothing ever comes of it. I pointed this out to the writers and the next day they presented me with a delicious scene that took care of the problem. I knew then this was a place I wanted to work.*
>
> RALPH SENENSKY, DIRECTOR

> *I was blessed to have gotten to play this wonderful character, Cissy Walker. I loved the episode where Cissy is trying to make Yancy jealous by flirting with John-Boy, and of course the episode where Cissy and Yancy get married. I loved every episode I appeared in: "The Chicken Thief," "The Baptism" "The Comeback," and "The First Casualty." There was always such wonderful writing, wonderful cast; Directors, and crew. Who could ask for more? Heck, let's do the whole thing again. This time I could be Grandma Cissy!*
>
> CISSY WELLMAN, ACTOR

Yancy Tucker (Robert Donner) and Cissy Walker (Cissy Wellman).

> *It was a lifetime ago, but it was just yesterday that I played Yancy. Of all the shows I did the fans seem to love this one the most. Yancy was always such a scamp. I think there is some scamp in all of us. In a way Yancy represented the dark side of all of us. He wasn't really bad. He was just kind of gray.*
>
> BOB DONNER, ACTOR (YANCY TUCKER)

The Prize

Air date: 10/25/73; Writer: Dale Eunson; Director: Philip Leacock
When the County Fair comes to Walton's Mountain, Grandma
enters the quilt competition and Ben sells a pig for the greased pig
contest. Olivia's childhood suitor, Oscar Cockrell, now running for
the state legislature, visits the fair and is obviously still smitten
with Olivia.

The Braggart

Air date: 11/01/73; Writer: Richard Fielder; Director: Jack Shea
The family greets Hobart Shank, a teenage orphan, who returns to
the Walton home after many years' absence. He informs John that
a baseball scout is coming to see him play and asks John to negoti-
ate his contract. He subsequently falls out of the tree house and
breaks his arm, losing his chance at baseball fame. Hobie accepts
the position of athletic instructor at the orphanage. The role of
Hobie is played by writer John McGreevey's son, Michael.

> *My main recollection of "The Braggart" is that the character of*
> *Hobie was so much fun to play. Loud, boisterous Hobie was a*
> *strapping country boy who could throw a baseball faster than*
> *Dizzy Dean and wasn't shy about telling the world that he was*
> *something special. On the surface, he was nothing like me, but*
> *deep down I connected with Hobie's insecurity and need to be*
> *loved. The day after the show aired, a young man approached me,*
> *and with tears flooding his eyes, thanked me for "telling his story."*
> *Like Hobie, he had been an orphan whose dreams of a career in*
> *professional baseball were ended by an arm injury.*
>
> MICHAEL MCGREEVEY, ACTOR (HOBIE)

The Fawn

Air date: 11/08/73; Writer: John McGreevey; Director: Ralph Waite
John-Boy secures the position of rent collector for Graham Foster,
a hated landlord, who treats his renters with disdain. Meanwhile,
Erin nurses an orphaned fawn, whom she names Lance, back to
health and struggles with her decision to place him back in the
wild on the mountain.

Ralph Waite directed this one. I remember it was his first time to direct the show. What I remember even more is that it was the first time I had to kiss a boy on screen. I was really very inexperienced and I was horrified. But it was just the beginning. For some reason the writers wrote in kissing scenes for me in just about every other show.

MARY MCDONOUGH, ACTOR (ERIN WALTON)

The Thanksgiving Story

Air date: 11/15/73 (two-hour episode); Teleplay: Joanna Lee; Story: Earl Hamner; Director: Philip Leacock

John-Boy anxiously anticipates a visit from his girlfriend, Jenny Pendleton, and his pending college scholarship exam. He is accidentally hit in the head by a board in the sawmill and his vision is blurred. He is unable to finish his test and eventually must undergo surgery. The Baldwin sisters request permission to adopt Ben but settle for Thanksgiving dinner. John-Boy passes his makeup exam arranged by Miss Hunter.

Mary McDonough (Erin) and Lancelot the fawn.

The Substitute

Air date: 11/22/73; Writer: John McGreevey; Director: Lee Philips
Miss Pollard, a substitute teacher from New York, is unsympathetic to the specific needs of the children. Ben enters a kite-flying contest and receives many unwanted suggestions on the proper design. After a talk with Olivia, Miss Pollard warms to the children and attends the kite-flying contest with the family. Ben wins second place.

The Bequest

Air date: 11/29/73; Writer: Mort Thaw; Director: Alf Kjellin
Grandma receives a letter stating that she has inherited $250. She announces to the family and the congregation at church that she will share her wealth. A few days later, she is informed that there was a mistake and she will actually receive nothing. Mary Ellen, envious of a fellow classmate, experiments with blonde hair coloring and uses Jim-Bob as a test case.

The Air-Mail Man

Air date: 12/13/73; Writers: Peter and Sarah Dixon; Director: Robert Butler
One evening a mail plane makes an emergency landing in the Waltons' meadow. The next day John helps the pilot repair the plane and Olivia receives a plane ride from the pilot as a surprise birthday present.

> *There always seemed to me to be a kind of fresh-air, sun-washed clarity about the show. I felt that the writing staff's ideas, their notions on character and humanity and fair play, were lucid and light, familiar and comforting, and easily accessible to all of us. The simplicity of the Walton life, its dignity and stature, the affection and love in those people, was deep and honest and even-handed always. Simplicity and honesty and the warm sunshine born of decency—that's the way I always felt whenever I worked on this series.*
>
> BOB BUTLER, DIRECTOR

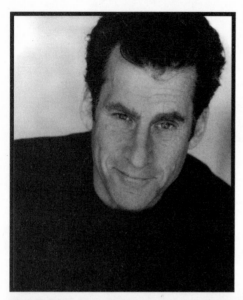

Paul Michael Glaser guest-starred in "The Air-Mail Man."

Elizabeth Walton, (Kami Cotler), Mary Ellen Walton (Judy Norton), and Erin Walton (Mary McDonough).

Paul Michael Glaser, best known for his leading role in Starsky and Hutch, *played the Air-Mail Man.*

EARL HAMNER, CREATOR AND EXECUTIVE PRODUCER

The Triangle

Air date: 12/20/73; Writer: Lionel E. Siegel; Director: Lee Philips
With Miss Hunter's encouragement, John-Boy enters an essay-writing contest while Ben sends for a bodybuilding course to increase his physique. Miss Hunter and Reverend Fordwick become a romantic couple, to John-Boy's dismay. Ben loses the nail-driving contest at the church picnic.

> *The best thing about filming* The Waltons *was that they let me bring my dog, Jake, to work. While doing a play in New York City, Jake had followed me home from the theater one night, so he returned with me to California. I don't know anything about his life before I met him, but the first time he was on the set with me and they called "Action!" he lay down and was perfectly still until the director called "Cut," at which time he'd jump up and shake hands. You can see him in some episodes. I never took him on any other set. Thank you, Harry Harris.*

> MARICLARE COSTELLO, ACTOR (ROSEMARY HUNTER FORDWICK)

The Awakening

Air date: 1/03/74; Writer: Joanna Lee; Director: Lee Philips
Grandma resents the signs of old age, while Mary Ellen has her first pangs of teenage love for a college boy. Mary Ellen and John-Boy compete for the shed as their own "private place." The family celebrates Grandma's sixty-eighth birthday, and Mary Ellen decides the shed isn't for her after all.

> *What actress doesn't remember her first screen kiss! Not only did I get kissed by one very attractive man, I was also given a dozen roses by another, my brother John-Boy Walton.*

> JUDY NORTON, ACTOR (MARY ELLEN WALTON)

The Honeymoon

Air date: 1/10/74; Writer: John McGreevey; Director: Jack Shea
The children are being particularly difficult and Olivia's patience

runs thin. John suggests they go on a belated honeymoon to Virginia Beach. John-Boy and Marcia Woolery try to come to an understanding in their relationship, and Grandma goes away to help a sick friend. After mishaps occur at home, Olivia and John return and John plans a camping trip for everyone.

The Heritage

Air date: 1/17/74; Writer: Dale Eunson; Director: Harry Harris
Charley Harmon approaches John to sell the mountain with its valuable mineral springs as a tourist and health center. The offer is generous and John seriously considers the sale. As Zeb and Esther's fiftieth anniversary approaches, each member of the family reflects on what their home means to them. John does not sell.

> *I found this episode very moving because each member of the family has to examine what the mountain means to them, and what each of them decides is that no price can be put on what they already own—their home on the mountain. The episode was special too because three of my favorite actors appeared in it: Robert Donner as Yancy Tucker, John Crawford as Sheriff Bridges, and Nora Marlowe as Mrs. Brimmer.*

> DUANE SHELL, FAN—LOS ANGELES, CALIFORNIA

The Gift

Air date: 1/24/74; Teleplay: Carol Evan McKeand; Story: Ray Goldup and Jack Hanrahan; Director: Ralph Senensky
Jason's friend Seth Turner (Ron Howard) has a fatal disease and learns that he has just one year to live. His father is a singer, and Seth's goal has always been to join his father in a musical career. Initially Jason is shocked at the news and can't bring himself to talk to his sick friend. John-Boy intercedes and helps Jason through this emotionally disturbing situation.

> *This episode was the work of the enormously talented writer Carol Evan McKeand. I considered it similar to what would be, in music, a tone poem. There is a tremendously moving scene where John-Boy asks Seth how he can so calmly face his approaching death. And the boy relates his feeling of acceptance. His words and acting are superb, but it is Richard, with his incredible gift of beautiful*

and compassionate reactions, without a word of dialogue, who steals the scene.

RALPH SENENSKY, DIRECTOR

One of my favorite episodes. Ron Howard played my best friend, Seth Turner, who was dying of leukemia. I had always been a fan of Ron's from The Andy Griffith Show, *and had grown up with people telling me I looked like him. When I first met Ron on the set, his first words were, "You're the guy everybody says I look like!" Ron later told me that "The Gift" was his favorite episodic performance, and that he had landed a starring role in* The Shootist, *John Wayne's last film, as a result of the producers' watching "The Gift."*

JON WALMSLEY, ACTOR (JASON WALTON)

Merle Haggard and Ron Howard starred in this one. Merle would sit and pick the whole day long. I was so in awe of him. I just loved his music, and here I was spending a week with the guy while he sits there picking.

I loved doing this show and I always enjoyed working with director Harry Harris. He was a delight. He knew what he wanted and he had a good time getting it. Come to think of it, I never had this kind of family, never had children, but this group of actors became my family and the Walton kids became my kids.

BOB DONNER, ACTOR (YANCY TUCKER)

Among the many well-known celebrities who appeared on The Waltons *is Ron Howard. Ron played the role of Seth Turner in this episode, and as this book was going to print he had just won the Best Director Oscar for* A Beautiful Mind.

EARL HAMNER, CREATOR AND EXECUTIVE PRODUCER

The Cradle

Air date: 1/31/74; Writer: Joanna Lee; Director: Ralph Senensky
Olivia becomes a door-to-door saleslady for a beauty cream. When she becomes ill she goes to Dr. Vance, who informs her that she is expecting. The children make her and the baby a variety of presents. Unfortunately, she loses the baby and everyone has to deal with disappointment.

Richard Thomas.

This is one of my favorite episodes, in which Olivia discovers she is pregnant and suffers a miscarriage. A week before this episode was shown originally, I also suffered a miscarriage. Seeing Olivia go through it and watching her family stand beside her helped me with my own loss. Since Olivia made it through this tragedy I knew I could too.

JENNI WISEMANN, FAN—MICHIGAN CITY, INDIANA

After a few short weeks of joy and expectation I too suffered a miscarriage. I was devastated and felt it was because of something I had done or not done. I listened to Grandma's, Grandpa's, and John's words of wisdom and gradually came to terms with my loss. I have been watching an episode of The Waltons *every day for the last twenty years. Since I saw the first episode in my early teens I wanted this way of family life. I never changed and went on to have six children. I have raised my family using* Waltons *episodes as guidelines and it is a way of life for me.*

TRACY BATCHELOR, FAN—SUSSEX, ENGLAND

The Fulfillment

Air date: 2/07/74; Writers: Michael Russnow and Tony Kayden; Director: Nick Webster
Stevie, an eight-year-old orphan child, is temporarily with the Waltons. The little boy is unhappy, and when he is reprimanded by Olivia he runs away and connects with blacksmith Curtis Norton. An immediate bond occurs. Curtis's wife, Ann, can't have children, and eventually Curtis and his wife take in the boy and plan to adopt him.

The Ghost Story

Air date: 2/14/74; Writer: Nigel McKeand; Director: Ralph Waite
The children play with a Ouija board and try to "speak to the spirits." The game spells out the name "Luke," which is the name of the

little boy staying with them. It further warns them that he should not take the train. The Waltons' truck breaks down on the way to the station and later they hear on the radio that the train Luke would've been on had crashed.

The Graduation

Air date: 2/21/74; Writer: Lionel E. Siegel; Director: Alf Kjellin

John-Boy receives a new suit of clothes in preparation for his high school graduation. Chance, the family cow, dies and John-Boy secretly returns the clothes to buy another cow for the family. He graduates in Grandpa's burial suit. John-Boy gives a speech at graduation and the family beams with pride.

The Five-Foot Shelf

Air date: 3/07/74; Writer: John Hawkins; Director: Ralph Waite

Jon Walmsley.

Olivia and John-Boy are convinced by George Reed, a traveling book salesman, to buy a five-foot collection of books known as the Harvard Classics. Instead of sending the $3 down payment to the home office, however, the salesman uses the money to buy his daughter a doll for her birthday. He is confronted by John and returns the doll to Ike and the down payment to Olivia, who decides to order the books anyway.

The Car

Air date: 3/14/74; Writer: Chris Andrews; Director: Philip Leacock

John-Boy is in the market for a used car to travel to and from college. Ike tells him that Hyder Rudge has a car he never uses. John-Boy makes a deal with Mr. Rudge to make repairs to Rudge's home in exchange for the car. As John-Boy works at the Rudge home, he becomes suspicious of Mr. Rudge, who hides the auto and refuses to sell it to John-Boy. Mrs. Rudge explains that the car belonged to their dead son and that her husband has an emotional attachment to the vehicle. In the end, John-Boy gets the car after all.

I was moved by the way in which the actors and Philip Leacock, the director, succeeded in making the viewer feel the parents' grief for their lost son. Through the excellent acting of Ed Lauter, we identified with a father who clings to the car in the futile hope that his son will return. Through the sensitive portrayal by Richard Thomas, we understood that John-Boy desperately needed the car to enable him to go to college. Subtly conveyed was the knowledge that both parents were helped by the resolution and their son's memory would live on in John-Boy.

CHRIS ANDREWS (A.K.A. MARILYN SIPES), WRITER

Season Three (1974–1975)

The Conflict

Air date: 9/12/74 (two-hour episode); Writer: Jeb Rosebrook; Director: Ralph Senensky

Aunt Martha Corinne Walton's home is in danger of being torn down because of the right-of-way for the Blue Ridge Parkway. Boone and Wade Walton come and ask for aid. They are not moving as the government has asked. The entire Walton family comes to her aid and tries to stop the construction. John-Boy is shot during a skirmish with the contractor and deputies. This is often listed as a favorite episode of the fans.

Jeb Rosebrook.

In the summer of 1952, while working for the Buildings and Grounds Department at the University of Virginia in Charlottesville, a coworker told me the story of his family having been forcefully evicted from their mountain home in the Blue Ridge to pave the way for the Skyline Drive. Twenty years later when I remembered this story, a mountain matriarch named Martha Corinne came to mind (I named her after two of my aunts). She was magnificently portrayed by Beulah Bondi, and the honesty of the story was made possible in part by research provided by Earl Hamner's mother. All in all this was a special writing experience, one that went so beautifully from the page to film.

JEB ROSEBROOK, WRITER

Goodnight John-Boy

Jeb's words also went beautifully from the page to the stage. In the fall of 1998 Jeb's stage play based upon his screenplay was performed by the Nelson County Drama Foundation. Set upon an outdoor stage on a mountainside not far from where the actual events took place, the drama was an unforgettable event. It was the brainchild of local citizen Jean Arey, whose vision it was to bring live theater to the area. The role of Martha Corinne was played by actress Karen Handley with extraordinary strength and dignity. Karen was notably supported by other gifted local actors. The performance was all the more poignant for many in the audience who were descended from those who had been removed from land their ancestors had cultivated and settled upon since pioneer times. In her stage notes Jean Arey said: "Realizing the magnitude of their loss, we better appreciate the debt we owe the families who gave up their lands and homesteads so the nation's longest linear park could be built. They bequeathed us a national treasure. That is why this production is dedicated to them."

EARL HAMNER, CREATOR AND EXECUTIVE PRODUCER

This episode will always be special to me because it introduced the incomparable Beulah Bondi into my life. I will always remember the elegant poetic closing scene between John-Boy and Martha Corinne. He has come to fetch her. It is time to leave her mountain home forever, and she is sweeping out the cabin for the last time. She intends to leave the place just as she found it on her wedding day. It was exciting to read. It was exciting to film. All in all a very special experience.

RALPH SENENSKY, DIRECTOR

Some episodes of The Waltons *we choose as favorites because of the way the story relates to our own lives. This was the way the story of Martha Corinne affected me. She looked and dressed the same as my grandmothers and great-grandmothers with her bonnet, black stockings, and big white apron. I just wanted to crawl up in her lap and be wrapped up in that apron and rocked one more time.*

My paternal great-grandparents built and lived in a one-room log cabin. Three rooms were added later. I lived with my parents in that little house for a while as a small child. Seeing the log cabin and surrounding area of Martha Corinne's cabin took me on a nostalgic trip home again.

JUNE ASH, FAN—ODENVILLE, ALABAMA

The First Day

Air date: 9/19/74; Writer: John McGreevey; Director: Philip Leacock
John-Boy's first day as a college student brings him a variety of new challenges at Boatwright University. He is harassed by upperclassmen. Back home, Jason feels the need to be the "oldest" and tries to excel at school as John-Boy did. The other children object to Jason's newfound attitude.

The Thoroughbred

Air date: 9/26/74; Writers: Michael Russnow and Tony Kayden; Director: Harry Harris
John-Boy enters the family mule, Blue, in the annual cross-country horse race and tries to win Selena Linville's affections. Grandpa had won the race years before and John-Boy hopes to continue in that tradition.

> *The whole family is excited when John-Boy sets to race Blue the mule against a thoroughbred horse. Blue was a stubborn critter and wouldn't allow me to "direct" him, just wouldn't move. So we brought in a substitute mule but he wouldn't move either. Someone suggested there was a camel back at the animal compound the mule was afraid of. We brought in the camel to prod the substitute into running, but he still wouldn't move. Somehow, John-Boy and Blue still win the race!*
>
> HARRY HARRIS, DIRECTOR

The Runaway

Air date: 10/03/74; Teleplay: Larry Bischof and Carol Evan McKeand; Director: Harry Harris
Jim-Bob runs away from home after the school's pet guinea pig dies while in his care. He tries to talk to the family but everyone is too busy to listen. John-Boy helps locate Jim-Bob, but in doing so misses an important presentation at Boatwright University. The two brothers sit at a restaurant, where John-Boy meets the university speaker.

*One of my favorite episodes. In it Jim-Bob brought home the
school guinea pig, Porthos, during a vacation. Aside from most of
his siblings making fun of his responsibility, everyone in the family
was too involved with their own activities and problems and no
one cared when Porthos died the first night. Jim-Bob's decision to
run away from home impacted them all, and when John-Boy
eventually found him and convinced him to come home, it was a
wonderful example of what, to me, The Waltons was all about—
family togetherness and love, no matter what.*

VICKY CHOUDHRY, FAN

The Romance

Air date: 10/10/74; Writer: Hindi Brooks; Director: Ivan Dixon
At John-Boy's urging, Olivia enrolls in a night-school art class.
The teacher makes romantic advances and visits Olivia at
home. Mary Ellen announces that she has decided to become a
doctor.

*I was on the set one day when Michael Learned said to the direc-
tor that if the only reason she was in the scene was to pour coffee
then please write her out of that scene. Ellen Corby chimed in a
"ditto" for herself. And it was done! I was elated to see the sensitivity of the production company to the need for a more positive
image of women.*

HINDI BROOKS, WRITER

The Ring

Air date: 10/17/74; Writer: Nigel McKeand; Director: Philip Leacock
Mary Ellen is attending a college dance and buys a used purse for
the event. She lies about finding a ring belonging to Mrs.
Breckinridge in the purse, intending to give it back following the
dance. She loses the ring in the college's restroom.

The System

Air date: 10/24/74; Writer: Jeb Rosebrook; Director: Harry Harris
John-Boy defends a fellow student and football player, Tom
Povich, who violates Boatwright University's honor code during a
history exam. He is observed by John-Boy, and another student

sees John-Boy, and thus John-Boy has no option but to turn in Tom. As it turns out, there were extenuating circumstances, and Tom is not expelled. Ben learns the hazards of smoking from Grandpa.

> *In the spring of 1954, during my freshman year at Washington and Lee University in Lexington, Virginia, the school was rocked by an Honor System scandal that involved some members of the varsity football team. This episode about a football player from Pennsylvania being brought up on Honor System charges at Boatwright University and defended by John-Boy was inspired by this event.*
>
> JEB ROSEBROOK, WRITER

The Spoilers

Air date: 10/31/74; Writer: Carl Ledner; Director: Jack Shea
A New York family moves to Walton's Mountain to escape the ravages of the Great Depression. Ted Hanover and his family cause havoc in the Waltons' household, and eventually Ted realizes his mistake and moves his misplaced family back to New York City.

The Marathon

Air date: 11/07/74; Writer: Nigel McKeand; Director: Ralph Senensky
John-Boy enters a seven-day dance marathon in Scottsville with a total stranger, Daisy Garner. What started as fun quickly becomes drudgery and Olivia comes to the rescue. Back home the children build a crystal radio and listen to the music from the marathon.

> *A friend of Producer Bob Jacks told me several years after his death that this had been his favorite episode. I remembered that before filming this episode he and I watched a screening of* They Shoot Horses, Don't They? *He told me that when he had been a producer at Twentieth Century Fox he had tried to option the property but had not been able to acquire the rights. So on* The Waltons *he finally had a chance to cover that wonderful craze of the Depression years—the dance marathon. When I was nine or ten, a marathon was staged in the small Iowa town where I lived. I went with my parents every weekend to see it. One Friday night I entered the weekly amateur contest (I played piano) and won*

First Prize—fifty cents! It was the Depression, don't forget. This is one of my favorite episodes too. Great performances by Richard Thomas and Deirdre Lenihan as Daisy. And exquisite photography by the masterful Russell Metty. I watched it recently and marveled, not only at how good it still is, but that it was shot in only six days!

RALPH SENENSKY, DIRECTOR

Rockfish, Virginia.

One of the pleasures of being a part of this series was that frequently events of the period were dramatized, usually with John-Boy's character being integrated into the event. I felt that this episode about marathon dancing was particularly well done.

JOE CONLEY, ACTOR (IKE GODSEY)

The Book

Air date: 11/14/74; Writer: Joseph Bonaduce; Director: Harry Harris.
Unknowingly, Olivia submits a collection of John-Boy's short stories to a "vanity" book publisher. John-Boy beams with pride and self-importance until he realizes the publisher is billing him for publishing the book. Jason secures a job with Bobby Bigelow and the Haystack Gang. The family goes to hear Jason play with the band.

The Job

Air date: 11/21/74; Writer: Nigel McKeand; Director: Ivan Dixon
John-Boy obtains a job reading to a young blind woman who is hostile toward him and the world in general. After visiting Walton's Mountain, the girl realizes she has much for which to be thankful. While on a picnic, Elizabeth falls off a bridge into Drucilla's Pond.

The Departure

Air date: 12/05/74; Writer: Joanna Lee; Director: Ivan Dixon
Feeling that life has passed him by, John seeks work in a Norfolk shipyard. He resides in a boarding house where other shipyard workers live. During a visit from John-Boy, they both end up in a fight. John soon realizes that the family needs him at home and he really wants to be there.

The Visitor

Air date: 12/12/74; Writer: Kathleen Hite; Director: Ralph Waite
Zeb's old friend, Mason Beardsley, mysteriously returns to Walton's Mountain without his wife. The family has a visit from his son, James Lee, who informs them that his mother died but his father will not acknowledge her passing.

The Birthday

Air date: 12/19/74; Writer: Nancy Greenwald; Director: Ivan Dixon
As Grandpa's seventy-third birthday approaches, he is stricken with a heart attack and seems to be unresponsive to treatment. To cheer him up, against doctor's orders, the family moves him to a tent outside so he can communicate with nature. The doctor is upset, but Grandma insists and wins the argument. Zeb immediately improves.

> *Many of the episodes I have watched so many times that I believe I know every word. I loved Grandpa Walton. His spunk, love, and positive outlook on life drew you to him. He accepted each person as they were and encouraged each to be his or her best. I was moved by this story about Grandpa's heart attack, one of the few times he needed an extra helping of love and concern.*
>
> CHRISTINE SEEK, FAN—NEWPORT BEACH, CALIFORNIA

The Lie

Air date: 1/02/75; Writer: Hindi Brooks; Director: Jack Shea
Ben borrows John-Boy's car without permission to take Nancy Madden, a classmate, to Charlottesville to meet her mother. Unknown to Ben, the car is involved in a hit-and-run accident. The driver of the other car takes down John-Boy's tag number and

the next day the sheriff makes a call. Initially Ben denies taking the car, but he eventually shares the whole Nancy Madden situation.

> *I loved using my own experience as a wife and mother when writing the series. One of my episodes called for Olivia to knit a sweater. She did it out of odds and ends of yarn, doubling up the thinner yarns when necessary. I did that in my knitting many times.*
>
> HINDI BROOKS, WRITER

The Matchmakers

Air date: 1/09/75; Writer: John McGreevey; Director: Jack Shea
Cousin Corabeth Walton, from Doe Hill, comes for an unexpected extended visit. Her takeover of John-Boy's room seems rather permanent. Ike Godsey is instantly taken with her and they quickly marry. With John-Boy's encouragement, Erin enters the Jefferson County Sweetheart Contest.

> *When I was given the role of Corabeth Godsey, I realized with my first show that I had been given a gift. Every actor wants a role where the person undergoes change and growth. Corabeth had many facets. She was often difficult and the audience couldn't bear her, and then she would redeem herself and the audience would be touched by her. This was due to insightful and beautiful writing. I believe it was the best-written role on the show.*
>
> RONNIE CLAIRE EDWARDS, ACTOR (CORABETH GODSEY)

> *It was always especially rewarding to feel that with an episode I had made some worthwhile and lasting contribution to* The Waltons. *The addition of Verdie Grant in "The Scholar" was one such show. "The Matchmakers" was another because it introduced Corabeth, who was to become (with many misgivings before and after the ceremony) Mrs. Ike Godsey. Corabeth, marvelously interpreted by Ronnie Claire Edwards, added a new dimension of comedy to the series. I was especially pleased a few years ago to attend a screening of "The Matchmakers" in a fairly large auditorium at the Los Angeles County Museum. There was continuous laughter.*
>
> JOHN MCGREEVEY, WRITER

Ronnie Claire Edwards gave such interest and depth to the character of Corabeth that we asked her to stay as a permanent member of the cast, and the series was much the richer for her presence. To acting Ronnie Claire has now added the chores of a producer and writer—her latest book, The Knife Thrower's Assistant, *is a hilarious read.*

EARL HAMNER, CREATOR AND EXECUTIVE PRODUCER

The Beguiled

Air date: 1/16/75; Writer: Kathleen Hite; Director: Ralph Senensky
John-Boy collides with Sis Bradford, a sassy but unprincipled girl, whose selfish ways cause hard feelings and suspicion toward Jim-Bob's friend Danny. Danny's father suspects that he took John-Boy's chemistry notebook, but Jim-Bob says he saw Sis take it.

The Caretakers

Air date: 1/23/75; Writer: Richard Carr; Director: Ivan Dixon
Grandpa and Grandma become angry with the family when they believe that everyone feels that they are old and worthless. They move out to care for a friend's house. To fill a lumber order, John hires Easy Jackson to fill in for Zeb. Everyone soon realizes that Grandpa's and Grandma's place is back home.

The Shivaree

Air date: 1/30/75; Writer: Max Hodge; Director: Lee Philips
Wedding plans for a friend's daughter go awry when the mountain custom of kidnapping the groom gets out of hand. The groom, Bob Hill from Richmond, is unfamiliar with the shivaree custom and becomes quite angry.

The Choice

Air date: 2/06/75; Writer: Nancy Greenwald; Director: Alf Kjellin
John decides to expand the mill and call it Walton and Sons, but Jason wants to study music and tries out for a scholarship at Kleinburg Conservatory of Music. Jason wins the scholarship and John comes to understand that music can be more than a hobby.

The Statue

Air date: 2/13/75; Teleplay: Earl Hamner; Story: Summer Long; Director: Ralph Waite

At a raffle at Godsey's store, Grandpa wins a statue donated by the Baldwin sisters. He places the statue in the front yard, but Grandma believes the statue has a remarkable resemblance to one of Grandpa's suitors prior to her and demands its removal. John-Boy writes a story about the failed romance between Miss Emily and Ashley Longworth. When he reads the story to the Baldwin sisters Miss Emily becomes quite disturbed and John-Boy changes the ending.

> *This was a funny show about Grandpa having to get rid of a statue because it resembled one of his old lady friends and it made Grandma jealous. He decided to sink the statue in Drucilla's Pond and the whole family went with him to be sure he kept his word. Will pushed the statue into the pond and was ad-libbing dialogue he made up, which was always good but drove the producers crazy because he was departing from the script, and the camera was whirling away, and to everybody's horror the statue popped right back up to the surface. It wouldn't stay under water no matter what we tried, so we finally had to shoot around it.*
>
> Mary McDonough, Actor (Erin Walton)

The Song

Air date: 2/20/75; Teleplay: Richard Carr and Armand Lanzano; Story: Richard Carr; Director: Richard Thomas

Ben falls in love with Sally Ann Harper, but she has eyes only for Jason, who convinces Bobby Bigelow to let Sally Ann sing his new song with the band. Ben becomes very jealous and refuses to attend the radio broadcast. Sally Ann dedicates the song to Ben and they finally get together. John and Grandpa enter a billiards competition at Ike's store.

> *I enjoyed working with Erin Moran of* Happy Days *fame, who played the role of Sally Ann Harper.*
>
> Mary McDonough, Actor (Erin Walton)

The Woman

Air date: 2/27/75; Writer: Hindi Brooks; Director: Harvey S. Laidman
It's John and Olivia's twentieth wedding anniversary and the children paint a picture of the house with each of them depicted. John-Boy falls in love with a visiting lecturer at Boatwright and decides to leave the mountain with her. At the railway station he experiences a change of heart and stays on the mountain.

> *When Earl called me and asked if I wanted to write a Waltons I have to confess that I had never seen an episode of the show. I didn't know what a city girl like me would have in common with these country folk. But I said yes, and I was sent several episodes and brought in to view several others. And as I watched I realized this wasn't a series about "hicks" as I had heard. It was about real people. It was as much about me as it was about them. I could relate to every character and every episode. It was so personal that I was able to integrate lines from a poem I wrote when I was in college that was published in my college literary journal, and it fit right in!*
>
> HINDI BROOKS, WRITER

The Venture

Air date: 3/06/75; Writer: Joseph Bonaduce; Director: Ralph Waite
John decides to expand his business by building a new mill. To meet a deadline for a big order, he works day and night and gets pneumonia while working during a rainstorm. Olivia finds him unconscious and he is rushed to the hospital. While visiting John at the hospital, Ike overhears a conversation between John and John-Boy about money. In a last-minute effort, John's friends finish the mill, but the family loses the big contract.

Season Four (1975–1976)

The Sermon

Air date: 9/11/75; Writer: Kathleen Hite; Director: Harry Harris
The Reverend Fordwick and Miss Hunter plan their wedding and honeymoon. Rev. Fordwick asks John-Boy to deliver the Sunday sermon, and Grandma enthusiastically provides John-Boy with

many Bible verses and teachings. Miss Hunter asks Olivia to act as the substitute teacher. Their tasks prove to be both enlightening and interesting.

> *I loved this episode because it gave Ellen Corby a role in which she could show off, and she played it to the hilt. Earl told me that when he first saw Ellen's performance he thought she was too grim, not at all like our two sweet-natured grandmothers. When he told her so she said, "Young man, you have got a bunch of saints in this show. Everybody is too sweet. I am going to give you a little vinegar." After that Earl says he did not advise her on interpreting her character again.*

MARION HAMNER HAWKES,
MODEL FOR MARY ELLEN

The Genius

Air date: 9/18/75; Writer: Robert Weverka; Director: Harry Harris

Dean Beck asks John-Boy to take care of Lyle Thomason, a sixteen-year-old genius college student, for the weekend. It seems that Lyle is brilliant in science and math but completely lacking when it comes to dealing with people.

The Fighter

Air date: 9/25/75; Writer: Andy White; Director: Ivan Dixon

James Travis Clark (Cleavon Little), a young prizefighter from Richmond, arrives on Walton's Mountain looking for work. He lives in the Waltons' barn while training for his next fight. Grandma and Olivia are upset with the whole idea until they find out that James is a minister. James loses the fight and is nursed back to health by Verdie Grant.

Marion Hamner Hawkes

The Prophecy

Air date: 10/02/75; Writer: Marion Hargrove; Director: Harry Harris
Eula Mae, a former classmate of John's, convinces him to attend the twenty-fifth reunion of the class of 1911. John is not at all thrilled with the prospect of his reunion, and he feels like a failure compared to his classmates. Eula Mae's plans fall apart and Olivia agrees to hold the reunion at home. During dinner, John finds out that he is admired and envied by his friends and classmates.

The Boondoggle

Air date: 10/09/75; Writers: Rod Peterson and Claire Whitaker; Director: Ralph Waite
Famous reporter Porter Sims arrives on Walton's Mountain to write a guide to Virginia. While going through Judge Baldwin's personal papers, he finds information that indicates the judge was accused of treason for harboring Union soldiers during the Civil War. The Baldwin sisters are horrified. Further investigation by John-Boy uncovers the fact that the judge ministered to the wounded on both sides.

> *We had always written separately but decided to team up to write our first episode for* The Waltons. *We focused on the Baldwin sisters and decided to give Miss Mamie a suitor. After all, Miss Emily had Ashley Longworth to moon over, and it seemed only fair to put a little romance into Miss Mamie's life. Rod's childhood memories of the Depression, coupled with some research, added color. We were elated to write for the series, and together we struggled fiercely with it. Later episodes we wrote benefited from this early learning period—and so did our relationship.*
>
> Rod and Claire Peterson, Writers

The Breakdown

Air date: 10/16/75; Writer: John McGreevey; Director: Ivan Dixon
Jason is constantly tired while burning the candle at both ends. He is attending Kleinberg Conservatory during the day and playing with Bobby Bigelow's Haystack Gang at night. He is doing nothing well and finally collapses. Olivia forces him to slow down. John-Boy takes a new job in Boatwright's library.

Jon Walmsley.

The Wingwalker

Air date: 10/23/75; Writer: Andy White; Director: Harvey S. Laidman
John-Boy writes a story on a female wing-walker who is performing at the local fair. He invites her to stay at the Walton home
instead of in town, and Jim-Bob is soon madly in love with her.
Maud Gormley gives Myrtle the goat to the Walton children.

The Competition

Air date: 10/30/75; Teleplay: Nancy Greenwald and Paul West; Story:
Nancy Greenwald; Director: Alf Kjellin
Chad Marshall, a handsome forestry student, arrives on Walton's
Mountain, and both Mary Ellen and Erin develop crushes on him.
A competition develops between the sisters, and Mary Ellen finally
realizes that Erin is truly in love. Olivia wants another child but
the doctor advises against it.

The Emergence

Air date: 11/06/75; Writer: Hindi Brooks; Director: Alf Kjellin
Marcia Woolery, one of John-Boy's old girlfriends, returns to
Walton's Mountain with her new boyfriend to sell some inherited

Judy Norton as Mary Ellen Walton.

property. She plans to invest the money in her boyfriend's proposed business. The boyfriend is arrogant and treats Marcia poorly. John-Boy exposes him as a braggart and not in love with Marcia. While substitute teaching, Olivia helps Samuel Miller, one of her students, obtain a pair of much-needed eyeglasses.

The Loss

Air date: 11/13/75; Writer: Joan Scott; Director: Alf Kjellin

Olivia's young cousin, Olivia Hill, who was married in the "Shivaree" episode, returns to the mountain to grieve the sudden death of her husband. The family attempts to cheer her up but to little avail until Elizabeth's cat, Calico, dies while having kittens. The young widow takes a turn for the better while tending to the litter of kittens.

The Abdication

Air date: 11/20/75; Teleplay: Matt Robinson and Paul West; Story: Matt Robinson; Director: Harvey S. Laidman

The Walton family intently follows the abdication of King Edward VIII while following the activities of a movie company filming on Walton's Mountain. John-Boy renews his friendship with A. J. Covington, the writer for the movie, who is working on location with the movie crew. John-Boy is asked to rewrite some scenes. He does so well his friend is fired and John-Boy is offered the job but declines.

> *This was an episode that really touched me. I loved that I got a firsthand history lesson from working on the series. So many of the real-life incidents that we covered enabled me to not only learn what happened but also to vicariously feel what people must have felt experiencing these events themselves. I thought the story of Edward and Wallis so romantic at the time, as well as a profound statement about priorities in life.*
>
> JUDY NORTON, ACTOR (MARY ELLEN WALTON)

The Estrangement

Air date: 12/04/75; Writers: Michael Russnow and Tony Kayden; Director: Harry Harris

Vera Walton leaves her husband, Wade, and moves into the Walton home. Wade has been abusive and is running moonshine. After Wade has a brush with the law, John offers him a job at the mill to help the young couple get on their feet and get back together. After a while, Wade earns enough money to open his own wood-carving shop.

The Nurse

Air date: 12/11/75; Writer: Kathleen Hite; Director: Alf Kjellin

Mary Ellen leaves home for the first time to pursue her dream of becoming a nurse. Before she leaves, the family showers her with surprise good-bye gifts. Although accepted at nursing school, she needs more work in math and science, so she studies with John-Boy and helps the county nurse, Miss Nora Taylor.

> *Mary Ellen, aspiring to fulfill her dream to become a qualified nurse, struggles to overcome the challenge of learning in a very different environment: a teaching hospital. Although meeting many setbacks she still finds time to help an impoverished mountain family and nurse a terminally ill mother through her final days. Though saddened by this tragedy, Mary Ellen learns much from it and it helps her become a stronger person.*
>
> Mr. J. Howard, Fan—Lancashire, England

The Intruders

Air date: 12/18/75; Writer: Seth Freeman; Director: Richard Bennett

An angry Ben leaves home just when John and Grandpa enter a competition with another lumber mill for a big contract. Not aware of the competition, Ben takes a job with the rival firm. Grandpa tricks the rival firm to float their lumber down the river while the Waltons' lumber is delivered first.

> *This episode is particularly special to me because, among other reasons, it was the first dramatic prime-time television script I ever wrote and because Earl had done something extraordinary in giving me the assignment to write it. Earl had read a spec half-*

hour comedy script on a plane flight to New York and he had seen enough of a glimmer of talent in the piece to write me an encouraging letter. The letter was great, but the extraordinary and really unusual act was that Earl and producer Bob Jacks and story editor Carol McKeand then gave a writer of an unproduced half-hour comedy a shot at an hourlong dramatic episode of an honored television series. Most producers don't do that. Pigeon-holing is the norm. In my subsequent producing career, I have tried to emulate them and give writers who can write opportunities in new forms.

I had always been attracted to the character of Grandpa Walton, and my first story featured Grandpa in a sly and canny Brer Rabbit–like turn, outsmarting some unscrupulous, rival loggers in the region of Walton's Mountain, and teaching the youngest kids a special reverence for the land and the forest in the process. I started writing with great enthusiasm, but before long I hit a snag, a scene I couldn't manage to invest with the special kind of inventiveness that made a Walton *episode a* Walton. *I solved the problem in a weird way. I pretended I was Earl! I tried to imagine how he would handle the scene, and immediately I found myself back at work again. What I had done, of course, was to engage my imagination—and find a way to turn off the self-conscious critical mode of thought that can inhibit any creative work.*

SETH FREEMAN, WRITER

The Search

Air date: 1/01/76; Teleplay: Paul West; Story: Ellen Corby; Director: Harry Harris

Following a detour, Olivia, Jim-Bob, and Elizabeth become lost on their way to visit friends in the next county. The three experience many challenges, including moonshiners. Jim-Bob saves the day using woodsman skills taught to him by Grandpa.

In this episode, Olivia, Jim-Bob, and Elizabeth are lost in the woods and threatened by a wild bear. For safety's sake, rather than use a real bear, the producers asked one of our extras to put on a bear suit. The only problem was, this particular extra couldn't get the bear walk right and made the bear look like a kind of prissy girl and not the least bit threatening. "Let me have a crack at it," I said, confident that I had what it took to pass as a realistic, macho bear. The extra was more than happy to get out of the suit. I put it on and began trying to think like a bear. The suit was heavy, hot and smelled like—well, like an old bear. I could only see where I was going by looking at the ground through the bear's mouth. I began arranging twigs and rocks on the ground to have a trail to follow. I was getting overheated, out of breath, and feeling very claustrophobic. After several takes, we finally had some "bear" footage that was deemed acceptable. When the show aired, the suit looked fine, but the bear was looking at the ground the whole time trying to follow the trail of twigs and rocks. So the next time you see this episode, look for the awkward-looking, near-sighted bear, stumbling through the bushes, trying to find his mark—that's me!

JON WALMSLEY, ACTOR (JASON WALTON)

The Secret

Air date: 1/08/76; Writers: Rod Peterson and Claire Whitaker; Director: Harvey S. Laidman

Jim-Bob questions whether he is a real Walton or adopted, and he and John-Boy search out the details of his birth. While searching county birth records, he finds that he was part of a set of twins and that his twin brother died at birth.

Since our favorite Walton *episodes had always been those that focused strictly on the family, we tried as often as possible to avoid bringing outside characters into the story. This episode gave us an opportunity to explore family dynamics as Olivia confronted a devastating long-buried memory: the loss of an infant, Jim-Bob's twin. We were disappointed to have the climactic scene, which had been written for the mother, reassigned to another*

Rod and Claire Peterson.

character, but in general we felt we accomplished what we had set out to do.

ROD AND CLAIRE PETERSON, WRITERS

The Fox

Air date: 1/15/76; Writer: Max Hodge; Director: Richard Thomas
Grandpa likes to recount his exploits with Teddy Roosevelt and the Rough Riders in the Spanish-American War. Surprisingly, Zeb balks at attending a reunion of the Rough Riders. Ben decides to go into business trapping and selling animal skins. John-Boy submits a Spanish-American War story to *Adventure Magazine* but the story is rejected.

The Burnout

Air date: 1/22/76 (two-hour episode); Writer: John McGreevey; Director: Harry Harris
The Waltons' home is almost destroyed in a fire, and the children must live temporarily with friends. All the children adjust to living away from home except for Elizabeth, who seems overcome by fear. John-Boy finds it difficult to begin the task of rewriting his lost novel.

> *In the fourth season, I wrote the two-hour episode when the Waltons' home is almost destroyed by fire. Again, there was a personal motivation in their story for me. Our older daughter, when she was eight years old, spent the night at a friend's house. She became ill, and her friend's parents were not there to comfort and reassure her. Shortly after that, our home caught fire in the night and we had to awaken our children and lead them down a narrow wooden stairway, flames visible at the bottom. For the rest of her childhood, our daughter refused to spend the night away from home. This memory had a strong influence on my characterization of Elizabeth's fear. Again, I had the challenge of giving each of the cast special experiences as a result of the family's enforced separation.*
>
> JOHN McGREEVEY, WRITER
>
> *This was an interesting episode for many reasons. One of the difficult things to make believable on screen is to show a fire without*

actually burning down the building. Our art director, Ed Graves, was so dedicated to the look of reality that he would go out in a truck and collect scorched lumber from burned-out buildings to lay over the existing house and give it the right look.

HARRY HARRIS, DIRECTOR

I will never forget the terror on each family member's face during the fire. They were totally devastated with the loss of their family home. Then the children had to live with neighbors while their home was being rebuilt, and it was hard being separated as a family during the renovation. However, it didn't take them long to regroup and move forward in spite of their hardship. What I loved most was how John-Boy understood his sister Elizabeth's fears caused by the fire and helped her cope by showing his compassion for her. It is how a brother and sister should be. This episode shows that a family can face tragedy and separation, yet manage a strong, supportive, and loving connection until they resolve their situation and come together again.

MRS. SAM HARRIS, FAN—FREDERICKSBURG, VIRGINIA

This episode epitomized the Waltons for me. Their house burns but as they struggle to rebuild it they also struggle to rebuild their lives, which have been shattered by the tragedy.

SARAH SUDLOW, FAN—KENT, ENGLAND

The Big Brother

Air date: 1/29/76; Writer: John McGreevey; Director: Ralph Waite
John-Boy meets a runaway girl at the bus station. She is twelve-year-old Muffin Maloney, who tells him that she was abused and is trying to get to her mother. John-Boy takes the girl home and she fools everyone but Grandpa. She is really a con artist and her grandfather is in the local jail.

The Test

Air date: 2/05/76; Writer: Kathleen Hite; Director: Harvey S. Laidman
After sewing some clothes for the Baldwin sisters, Olivia is offered a job by Stella Lewis, a dressmaker in Rockfish. She does very well and soon there is talk of full-time work. She is pleased with the recognition but soon realizes that she wants to be home more than

at work. Maud Gormley's son, Leonard, puts his mother into an old folks' home. She loses her zest for life and returns to her own home.

The Quilting

Air date: 2/12/76; Writers: Rod Peterson and Claire Whitaker; Director: Lawrence Dobkin

The mountain custom of holding a "quilting" was to announce that a woman was of marrying age. Grandma is determined to have one for Mary Ellen, who is just as determined not to participate in what she considers an insulting custom. John-Boy intercedes and convinces Mary Ellen to cooperate with Grandma.

> *As time passed for the Walton family, we took note of the fact that Mary Ellen was approaching marriageable age. We asked ourselves if perhaps there shouldn't be some sort of ritual on the mountain to mark that occasion. Claire remembered her Utah neighbors gathering to make a quilt for every new bride in the community, and it seemed like the perfect way to announce to the world that Mary Ellen Walton was available for marriage. We knew Mary Ellen would hate the idea and that provided us with the conflict that made the episode so memorable.*
>
> ROD AND CLAIRE PETERSON, WRITERS

> *The program encompasses for me all that is good. The love, compassion, and humor that emanate from the family are like the quilt was for Mary Ellen. It would wrap around and provide comfort, love, and fond memories for many years to come as the Walton family has for me.*
>
> SHAIRON ANDREW, FAN—MANCHESTER, ENGLAND

The House

Air date: 2/19/76; Writer: Kirby Timmons; Director: Harvey S. Laidman

Grandma garners support to save from demolition an old house to which she has an emotional attachment. Zeb and John want the contract to tear it down for the old wood. The two argue until Grandpa realizes the house holds sentimental memories for Esther. The men win and the home is demolished. Grandpa installs a stained-glass window from the old home in his bedroom. Jason gives a musical recital based on Virginia folk songs.

The Fledgling

Air date: 2/26/76; Writer: Earl Hamner; Director: Harry Harris
John-Boy is offered an incredible opportunity to buy a printing press from the retiring local newspaper editor. He desperately tries to raise the down payment by working at the bus station. He loses his job when the former employee he is substituting for returns. John-Boy returns home to find the press in the shed, thanks to the generosity of the newspaper editor and his college professor.

The Collision

Air date: 3/04/76; Writer: John McGreevey; Director: Richard Thomas
Selena Linville returns to Walton's Mountain and stays with her grandfather, Colonel Linville. She encourages John-Boy to go with her to Europe and write about the war in Spain. She then learns that her grandfather is bankrupt and decides to stay and help him. She transfers to Boatwright to be closer to home.

> *Two episodes illustrate what happened to the United States in the late thirties and early forties and, thus, was happening on Walton's Mountain. The outside world beyond Walton's Mountain is becoming more and more inescapable. In "The Collision," a romantic young woman encourages John-Boy to go and fight in the Spanish Civil War (the "dress rehearsal" for World War II). In "The Hideaway," World War II is a brutal reality, and the refugee "heroine" brings some of the horror to rural Virginia.*
>
> JOHN MCGREEVEY, WRITER

Season Five (1976–1977)

The First Edition

Air date: 9/23/76; Writer: John McGreevey; Director: Lawrence Dobkin
John-Boy observes a local judge in an auto accident and decides to publish the story in the first edition of the *Blue Ridge Chronicle*. Olivia becomes angry with John-Boy when he publishes a story about his brother Ben, but John-Boy insists on impartiality.

The banner of the *Blue Ridge Chronicle*, John-Boy's newspaper.

Rockfish • Scottsville • Walton's Mountain • Lovingston • Charlottesville

THE BLUE RIDGE CHRONICLE

VOL. 1   TO SEARCH FOR THE TRUTH   8 Pages   THREE CENTS

The Vigil

Air date: 9/30/76; Writer: Kathleen Hite; Director: Harry Harris
Aspiring nurse Mary Ellen makes a wrong diagnosis about Grandma's illness that endangers Esther's life. Dr. Vance decides to leave Walton's Mountain. Meanwhile, Erin goes to work as a part-time assistant to Fanny Tatum, the telephone operator.

> *When I was cast as Miss Fanny Tatum, the Walton Mountain switchboard operator, I had never seen an old-fashioned telephone switchboard before except in the movies. Harry Harris was directing and he brought in someone to show me how to operate it. It was a forbidding-looking thing, and the instructor said, "You plug this in here when you are listening, and you plug this thing in this hole when you want to talk. And you plug these cords together when you're trying to connect two callers." Just looking at the thing made me nervous. Well, the camera started rolling and I couldn't remember which receptor was for listening and which one was for talking and I got it totally mixed up, but nobody seemed to notice the difference so I just kept on merrily as if I knew what I was doing. To make matters worse, everybody on Walton's Mountain seemed to have two names, like "Mary Sue" or "Sally Louise"! Still it was fun, and I enjoyed working with a great group of actors and directors.*
>
> SHEILA ALLEN, ACTOR (MISS FANNY TATUM)

The Comeback

Air date: 10/07/76; Writer: Seth Freeman; Director: Harvey S. Laidman

Jason receives the news that his scholarship at Kleinburg has been canceled, and he looks for a job to earn money for his tuition. He begins to play the piano at the Dew Drop Inn. Jason tries to interest Red Turner, a musician, into making a comeback since his son's death.

Sheila Allen as Miss Fanny Tatum, telephone operator.

> *This was a sequel to "The Gift." Country music legend Merle Haggard played Red Turner, father of Seth Turner, the character previously played by Ron Howard. It was great working with Merle and playing music on the set with him between takes. Merle was as humble and down-to-earth as he was talented. Years later, when I was working in Nashville, songwriters would tell me how envious they were that I had had the opportunity to meet and work with Merle.*

JON WALMSLEY, ACTOR (JASON WALTON)

The Baptism

Air date: 10/14/76; Writer: Andy White; Director: Ralph Waite

A famous evangelist visits Walton's Mountain. Yancy, Ben, and Corabeth are baptized in Drucilla's Pond, but John refuses in spite of Olivia's determined efforts.

The Firestorm

Air date: 10/21/76; Writers: Rod Peterson and Claire Whitaker; Director: Ralph Senensky

John-Boy, trying to keep the community informed about the news in Europe, decides to print excerpts from Hitler's *Mein Kampf* in his newspaper. A great outcry ensues, and the town is torn apart over the issue of publishing unfavorable items in the *Blue Ridge Chronicle*. Reverend Fordwick holds a book-burning in protest of Hitler.

Of all the episodes this was our favorite. A classic!

NANCY HAMNER JAMERSON, MODEL FOR ELIZABETH WALTON,

AND GARNETT JAMERSON

In the stories we wrote, we liked to make the Waltons a part of the times. When Rod was in high school in the late thirties, he had a social studies teacher who told the class about Adolf Hitler's book Mein Kampf. The teacher was criticized for "teaching" Nazism, and many of the local folks wanted him to be fired. This became the story of John-Boy's writing an editorial about the book, which turned into a book-burning on Walton's Mountain—and the near burning of a copy of the Bible in German!

ROD AND CLAIRE PETERSON, WRITERS

This episode teaches how judging can destroy people. Hitler was judging the Jews, and Walton's Mountain people were judging the Germans. Even poor Mrs. Brimmer was afraid to speak her native language. I truly respected how John-Boy stood firmly on his convictions that we should be able to read whatever is published whether we disagree with it or not. When they realize that they were about to burn the German Bible, the reality of misjudgment became very clear to all who were present. This episode teaches us to be more tolerant of the rights of others, even if we disagree with their philosophy.

MRS. SAM HARRIS, FAN—FREDERICKSBURG, VIRGINIA

When I first saw this episode, the moment when Mrs. Brimmer began to read Genesis 1:1 from the Bible resonated very clearly to me the message that human ignorance and narrow-mindedness can wreak havoc in any community. As members of society we need to make an effort to understand and become informed before we allow our emotions to control us. The Waltons dealt with this timeless issue before the renewed interest in the Holocaust began and did so in a very natural and poignant way.

NED FARNSWORTH, FAN—LIBENZELL MISSION, ECUADOR

The Night Walker

Air date: 10/28/76; Writer: Paul West; Director: Harvey S. Laidman

Lorin Hadley, a mysterious presence, prowls through the night on Walton's Mountain. Ike Godsey opens Godsey's Hall and Jason decides to have a dance for the community.

The Wedding

Air date: 11/04/76 (two-hour episode); Writers: Rod Peterson and Claire Whitaker; Director: Lawrence Dobkin

To her parents' surprise, Mary Ellen announces that she will marry Dr. David Spencer. As the family makes preparations, a new doctor, Curt Willard, arrives and complicates matters, ultimately marrying Mary Ellen.

> *We were thrilled to be invited to write the two-hour episode in which Mary Ellen fell in love and was married. In earlier episodes she had a beau, and it was expected that they would marry, but as we worked on it the story took another twist, almost of itself, and before we were finished she had met and fallen in love with Curt Willard, someone entirely different. We were gratified that the actor who was written out—the rejected suitor—went on to become a leading man in the daytime soaps.*
>
> ROD AND CLAIRE PETERSON, WRITERS

The Cloudburst

Air date: 11/11/76; Writer: Paul Cooper; Director: Harry Harris

To meet payments on his printing press, John-Boy sells "John-Boy's Meadow" to Bill Shelby, who supposedly represents a land company. Ike and Corabeth follow suit. However, what everyone does not know is that the company plans to strip mine, which will ruin the land. John-Boy stops the mining company, but that piece of land was never again to belong to the family.

> The Waltons *became responsible for my career when Earl graciously agreed to read a beginner's material and then offered enormous encouragement to this fledgling writer by opening doors and dispensing an untold bounty of both literary and career advice. His door was open widest and I was determined to write something he would buy for* The Waltons. *My wife, a former air force nurse, reminded me that Mary Ellen was a nurse. "What if Mary Ellen delivers a baby all by herself?" she asked. It was a wonderful notion. I stole it, wrote it, and submitted it and will never forget the fateful moment when Earl called and said, "Come in, let's talk."*
>
> PAUL COOPER, WRITER

The Great Motorcycle Race

Air date: 11/18/76; Writer: John Joseph; Director: Richard Thomas
Jim-Bob, a natural rider, enters a motorcycle race using Ike's old motorcycle, which he fixes up. Ike and Corabeth decide to adopt a baby, but bring home Aimee Louise, a young girl from the orphanage. Corabeth and Aimee have a difficult adjustment but work out everything in the end.

David Harper as Jim-Bob Walton.

I had watched The Waltons *from the time I was six or seven years old, so it was a big thrill when at eleven I was cast as Aimee Louise Godsey, the adopted daughter of Ike and Corabeth. I will always remember coming on set the first day and the first thing I laid eyes on was Will Geer in his overalls and I was speechless. My first scene was when Ronnie Claire and Joe introduced me to the Walton family. I was shy with them and tongue-tied, but that worked in the scene because I was supposed to be playing a waif-like creature. I remained on the show for the next four seasons, and even today when I see one of the actors we greet each other like family.*

RACHEL LONGAKER, ACTOR
(AIMEE GODSEY)

The Pony Cart

Air date: 12/02/76; Writer: Jack Miller; Director: Ralph Senensky
Aunt Martha Corinne Walton, Zeb's sister-in-law, comes for a visit and soon interrupts everyone's life. She helps Ben repair and paint an old-fashioned pony cart. Olivia finally gets fed up and indicates to Martha Corinne that she must go. While taking her home, John-Boy discovers that she is dying and takes her back to Walton's Mountain. After her death, she is buried in the family cemetery next to her husband, Henry.

Goodnight John-Boy

What a joy this episode was. What a joy to work with Beulah Bondi!

ERIC SCOTT, ACTOR (BEN WALTON)

I love this episode. Beulah Bondi does a fabulous job and she justly deserved to win the Emmy for her performance. She reminds me of my grandmother, and I think that may be a clue to the popularity of the show—a person or an event somehow reminds us of a person or an event in our own lives and the stories become very personal.

DUANE SHELL, FAN—LOS ANGELES, CALIFORNIA

I have so many stories about Beulah Bondi relating to this episode, it could take an entire chapter to tell them all. My favorite: After we finished filming "The Conflict," I bought my first VCR machine. And when the show aired, I taped it. During the following two years, I watched it many times. During this period I saw much of Beulah socially. She came to my house. I went to hers. And I remember that when I was with her personally, I could not see any trace of Martha Corinne. And when watching the tape, the actress and her character were so different I couldn't see any thing of the Beulah I had come to know. And then, the sequel, "The Pony Cart," brought Martha Corinne back to Walton's Mountain. The first morning of shooting I was on the back lot when across the lawn came this small figure, hurrying toward me, an old-fashioned bonnet on her head and a big smile on her face, and I smiled right back. It was Martha Corinne. And we greeted each other as two people would who had not seen each other in two years. I swear, that's the way it happened.

RALPH SENENSKY, DIRECTOR

With a masterly portrayal by Beulah Bondi and a poignant script filled with evocative imagery, "The Pony Cart" deals with the paradox of endings and continuity, death and life. In a tremendously moving climax, Martha Corinne, among her beloved Appalachian wildflowers, takes her final breath of sweet mountain air, completely at peace and at one with nature, completing her earthly pilgrimage.

RICHARD BOND, FAN—SUNDERLAND, ENGLAND

The Best Christmas

Air date: 12/09/76; Writer: John McGreevey; Director: Lawrence Dobkin

Olivia looks forward to this Christmas, the last when everyone will be together, and vows that this will be "the best Christmas." The weather, however, does not cooperate. Zeb and Esther are stranded in Charlottesville, a tree falls through the church roof, and Miss Fanny Tatum crashes into a pond. The family is scattered until Christmas morning, when they gather around the tree and sing hymns.

> *I treasure this episode because it marked one of the final episodes in which the entire original cast appeared together. I work in Ecuador at a mission where I am coordinator of children's ministries. I am far from my own family back home in Pennsylvania, and I think that the distance from them makes this episode so special to me.*
>
> NED FARNSWORTH, FAN—LIBENZELL MISSION, ECUADOR

The Last Mustang

Air date: 12/16/76; Writer: Calvin Clements Jr.; Director: Walter Alzmann

Ep Bridges has been the sheriff for fifteen years, but he is running in this election against a flamboyant opponent. Zeb fights to release a wild mustang that he says was caught on Walton land and belongs to the family. The mustang escapes and is recaptured by Zeb, branded with the Walton name, and released into the wild. With John-Boy's help, Ep wins the election.

The Rebellion

Air date: 12/23/76; Writer: Kathleen Hite; Director: Harvey S. Laidman

Olivia is obviously bored with her life and in a weak moment allows Corabeth to give her a permanent that turns her hair very curly. Meanwhile, Grandma experiences competition from Zelda Maynard for playing the church organ. Verdie shows Olivia how to put a "wrap" on her hair.

The Ferris Wheel

Air date: 1/06/77; Writers: Rod Peterson and Claire Whitaker; Director: Lawrence Dobkin

While Ben worries about being short, Elizabeth has nightmares involving a Ferris wheel. Ben buys elevator shoes to appear taller but no one seems to notice, and Elizabeth's visions lead to the recovery of some jewelry belonging to the Baldwin ladies.

> *Honest to gosh, Claire was in the early stages of sleep one night and dreamed the entire main plot. There was Elizabeth in her nightgown on the Ferris wheel. There was the thief who made off with the Baldwin sisters' jewels. It unfolded as if she was watching it on screen. In the subplot—which unlike the main plot took a lot of conscious thought—Ben, unhappy that Jim-Bob has outgrown him, proved that you don't need to be six feet tall to be a hero; something we thought would resonate with our audience. We visited the set during the filming and were awestruck to see that something that started as a dream resulted in a whole carnival on the Warner Brothers back lot.*
>
> ROD AND CLAIRE PETERSON, WRITERS

> *Being on the series provided me with many adventures. I swam in a pond with real beavers. I dangled from a harness eight feet in the air filming the dream sequence for the Ferris wheel. I was treed by hogs. Rode horses. Spoke my lines while Myrtle the goat butted me. On camera, I fell out of the tree house (fourteen feet!) and received a nasty, egg-sized bump on the back of my hard head. I got to ride in parades and answer phones on telethons. I worked with actors and crew members who had phenomenal past experiences. Met all kinds of fascinating people. Burned things, built things, and blew things up with schoolteacher Glen Woodmansee in the school trailer. All in all, a pretty good childhood!*
>
> KAMI COTLER, ACTOR (ELIZABETH WALTON)

> *This was a fun episode to do. I especially liked doing my own "stunt" and getting to go up on the real Ferris wheel to "save" Elizabeth.*
>
> ERIC SCOTT, ACTOR (BEN WALTON)

Kami Cotler as Elizabeth Walton.

The Elopement

Air date: 1/13/77; Writer: Hindi Brooks; Director: Harry Harris
Chad Marshall returns to the mountain, buys a piece of land, and asks Erin to marry him. She enthusiastically agrees, but John will not give his permission and says that Erin must wait until she graduates from high school. The couple plan to elope. Jason, filling in for Ike at the store, learns some fine points about store credit from Maud Gormley.

This time I not only had to kiss the guy, I eloped with him!

MARY McDONOUGH, ACTOR (ERIN WALTON)

This was the last episode in which Ellen Corby appeared before having her stroke.

EARL HAMNER, CREATOR AND EXECUTIVE PRODUCER

John's Crossroad

Air date: 1/20/77; Writers: Andy White and Paul West; Director: Richard Thomas
Little work is coming into the mill, so John applies for a construction-related office job in Charlottesville. He immediately has a run-in with his new boss, the office manager, Mr. Morgan. Grandpa takes Elizabeth to investigate a family of beavers, and they both fall into the pond and get full of mud. Olivia scolds them both about Elizabeth turning into a "tomboy."

> *I can't recall much of this episode except that I played a disagreeable character. Still* The Waltons *has been so much a part of my life for years that it's hard to believe I wasn't actually in the family. In a way I was.*

DONALD MOFFATT, ACTOR (MR. MORGAN IN THIS EPISODE)

The Career Girl

Air date: 1/27/77; Writer: Kathleen Hite; Director: Harry Harris
Erin is disappointed in herself when she realizes that she is the first Walton child to graduate from high school with no career plans for the future. John-Boy is in desperate need of a typewriter in order to professionally submit his manuscript about the mountain to a publisher.

The Hero

Air date: 2/03/77; Writer: Kathleen Hite; Director: Tony Brand
Still in the hospital, Grandma is unable to help John-Boy make preparations for her idea for Honor Day, a day celebrating the end of WWI. John-Boy conducts research in Richmond at the Red Cross and discovers that Sheriff Ep Bridges was a decorated hero. Ben touches Zeb's heart when he makes a memorial bench in honor of his uncle Ben killed in the war.

> *I was cast as Sheriff Ep Bridges of Jefferson County in the very first episode and enjoyed working in every one I was in, but the*

highlight of the episodes to me was this one. It was an opportunity for the sheriff to shine. Looking back, I can say that from the time I took the job my life and my career changed. People would come up to me on the street and comment on my work. My price went up along with my stature. The show changed my life. It's as simple as that.

JOHN CRAWFORD, ACTOR (SHERIFF EP BRIDGES)

The Inferno

Air date: 2/10/77; Writers: Rod Peterson and Claire Whitaker; Director: Harry Harris

In 1937, John-Boy wins a National Press Services award and is invited to cover the landing of the German dirigible *Hindenburg*. He meets fellow reporter Stewart Henry and together they view the horror of the explosion and fiery crash of the airship. Curt and Mary Ellen learn how to use a potted plant to gain much-needed privacy.

One of the aspects of working on the series was that it was faithful to the time in which it was set. It not only helped create a sense of reality, but it allowed us to dramatize events that took place during those years. In making this episode we integrated live action with film of the actual burning of the Hindenburg. *It made for a powerful and vivid episode.*

HARRY HARRIS, DIRECTOR

In this story John-Boy wins a prize for his editorial on Mein Kampf *and goes to Lakehurst, New Jersey, to report on the landing of the* Hindenburg *dirigible. With the skill of our film editor, we showed John-Boy seemingly present at this shocking moment as the giant airship burst into flames and crashed—as shown on old newsreel footage of the actual event. John-Boy was in such a state of shock that he could neither talk nor write about it. Later his father helped John-Boy work out his writer's block.*

ROD AND CLAIRE PETERSON, WRITERS

The Heartbreaker

Air date: 2/17/77; Writer: Seth Freeman; Director: Ralph Waite

Vanessa, Dr. Curt Willard's sister, arrives on Walton's Mountain and soon captures Jason's heart. She wants a singing career and is offered a job at the Dew Drop Inn singing with Jason. In an effort to increase circulation, John-Boy begins to print sections of his novel in the *Blue Ridge Chronicle*.

> *Jason falls in love with Curt Willard's sister, Vanessa, played by Linda Purl. Linda is a terrific actress and lots of fun to work with. In one scene I was serenading her on my guitar in a rowboat in the middle of Drucilla's Pond. Between takes we had to row back to shore to change the batteries in our radio mics. Linda had one foot on the dock and the other in the boat when the boat began to drift away. Her feet were getting farther and farther apart. I shifted to the other side of the boat to balance the weight just as Linda took a giant step backward. The boat flipped. We both went into the pond—in makeup, full wardrobe, wearing our radio mics, and me carrying an antique pocket watch given to me by my new girlfriend, Lisa, and clutching my 1958 Martin guitar. After lunch and a change of clothes, we resumed shooting. The guitar, which had been air-dried by the prop man, was fine, as was the pocket watch, though I never did find out the fate of those microphones!*
>
> JON WALMSLEY, ACTOR (JASON WALTON)

The Long Night

Air date: 2/24/77; Teleplay: Rod Peterson and Claire Whitaker; Story: Rod Peterson, Claire Whitaker, and Katharyn Power; Director: Harry Harris

Grandpa mistakenly announces to the family that he will be bringing Grandma home from the hospital. The doctor explains that it is too soon for Esther to check out, Zeb makes a scene, and the doctor denies him future visiting rights. Aimee Godsey, unhappy with Ike and Corabeth, runs away to the Walton home and emotionally asks Zeb to be her adoptive grandpa.

The Hiding Place

Air date: 3/03/77; Writer: John McGreevey; Director: Walter Alzmann

The Baldwin sisters invite the Waltons to a reception in honor of Hilary Baldwin von Kleist, who is visiting from war-threatened Vienna. John-Boy upsets the affair by asking questions about Hitler. Over Olivia's objections, Jason joins the National Guard.

Left, Will Geer as Grandpa Zeb Walton. *Below,* The Baldwin sisters, Mamie and Emily, played by Helen Kleeb and Mary Jackson.

In this story a relative of the Baldwin sisters arrives from her home in Vienna. She is Hilary Baldwin von Kleist, a woman of mystery. During her visit it is discovered she is fleeing hatred that resulted in the death of her son in pre–World War II Germany. Feeling it his duty in the shadow of approaching war, Jason joins the National Guard. Hilary was played by Jean Marsh, who starred in and co-produced the distinguished British TV miniseries Upstairs Downstairs. *The voices of President Franklin Roosevelt and Edward R. Murrow were supplied by Walter Edminston.*

EARL HAMNER, CREATOR AND EXECUTIVE PRODUCER

The Go-Getter

Air date: 3/10/77; Writers: Andy White and Paul West; Director: Lawrence Dobkin

Brothers Ben and John-Boy have an argument over Ben's work habits, leading to Ben leaving the newspaper and taking a new job as a used-car salesman. Sara Griffith visits the mountain, and Olivia takes her to Rockfish in hopes of meeting Sheriff Ep Bridges. Ben seems a natural salesman until the family learns about some of his questionable techniques and begins to doubt his honesty.

The Achievement

Air date: 3/17/77; Writers: Dale Eunson, Earl Hamner, and Andy White; Director: Harry Harris

John-Boy submits his completed novel to Hastings House Publishing in New York City. Impatient with their lack of response, he visits the publishers, where he meets Belle Becker, an editor, who promises to read his manuscript over the weekend. His persistence pays off, and he receives an offer to publish the novel with a request to prepare a second book. The exuberant John-Boy returns home with the good news, but also announces to the family that he will be living in New York City. This was the last episode in which Richard Thomas appeared as a regular cast member.

Saying good-bye to John-Boy, Grandpa, and Mama was like truly saying good-bye to family members. I missed their presence on the show and in my life very much.

JUDY NORTON, ACTOR (MARY ELLEN WALTON)

This episode was most touching. I doubt if there was a dry eye in the audience when John-Boy announces he is leaving Walton's Mountain. I suspect all families have a family member leave home at some time or other, and somehow this episode captures what we all feel at that time.

DUANE SHELL, FAN—LOS ANGELES, CALIFORNIA

I grew up with Mama serving supper in a dress and apron while I sat with my brothers and sisters on a bench at the kitchen table. I wore pigtails and sometimes went barefoot. These are just a few of the things on The Waltons *that I can personally relate to and a small part of what has made the series so dear to me.*

The minute I hear the theme song I am transported back to a Thursday evening at eight o'clock. I was taken into another world, a world of love, laughter, tenderness, and caring. That first episode will always have a special place in my heart, but dear to my heart also is "The Achievement," in which John-Boy, having announced he is moving to New York, walks across the yard, turns and looks at the house, and realizes that something momentous has happened and that nothing will ever be the same again. I remember my own big step from home to the city forty years ago and a tear trickles down my cheek. I can relate to what he is feeling.

KAY C. DISHER, FAN

There came a time in our family when someone was always leaving home. The girls left to go to school, or to jobs or to get married. All of us boys left at one time or another to go into military service. What made this episode so moving was the writing and Richard Thomas's acting. Each of the grownups reacts when they realize John-Boy is leaving for good, and each one, John, Olivia, Grandpa, and Grandma, has one final word with him. There is a point where he is all alone in the yard and he looks up to the house and says, "Goodnight, everybody." To me it was one of the most moving scenes in the entire series.

PAUL HAMNER, MODEL FOR BEN WALTON

Season Six (1977–1978)

The Hawk

Air date: 9/15/77; Writer: Andy White; Director: Tony Brand
Olivia, Sarah, and Corabeth travel to Boatwright University to select a new minister for Walton's Mountain. They choose Hank Buchanan, a handsome young minister, who causes some uneasiness within Corabeth, who is smitten with his good looks. John and Hank participate in Yancy's poker game. The congregation is unsettled, and John advises the young minister to fight for his career and confront his critics.

The Stray

Air date: 9/22/77; Writer: Kathleen Hite; Director: Harry Harris
The family finds Josh, a twelve-year-old runaway black boy, hiding in the barn. The young boy falls in love with the family and they with him but everyone knows he can't stay. Verdie and Harley decide to adopt Josh. Meanwhile, everyone has to deal with Jim-Bob's lack of attention. Elizabeth says, "His head is on vacation."

Nancy Hamner Jamerson

> *This was the story that introduced the character of Josh to the series. For a while, before he was adopted by Verdie and Harley Foster, Josh was taken in by the Walton family, where he attached himself to John Walton. I remember John buys the little boy a pair of shoes and they bond together the way Daddy would have done with any child (black or white, he was not prejudiced). The way John's character was written and acted it reminded me so much of my own father that this is my favorite episode.*

NANCY HAMNER JAMERSON, MODEL FOR ELIZABETH

The Recluse

Air date: 9/29/77; Writer: Seth Freeman; Director: Walter Alzmann
When the used-car lot is closed, Ben finds himself out of work and goes to Norfolk to work at a shipyard. Back home Jason meets Fern Lockwood, who shares his love of music. Fern is a widowed recluse, but with the family's help she comes out of her "shell." Ben eventually returns home to help his overworked father in the mill.

The Warrior

Air date: 10/13/77; Writer: Joan Scott; Director: Ralph Senensky
Two Cherokee Indians, a grandfather and grandson, show up on Walton's Mountain claiming the barn is built on sacred burial grounds. The grandfather demands that the barn be torn down. John refuses. Later that night, the grandfather sets the barn on fire. During his trial, the grandfather collapses and dies. Zeb agrees that the old man can be buried on a special place on the mountain.

> *Some shows were more of a challenge than others. Sometimes what went on behind the camera was as dramatic as the action in front of the lens. Such was the case with "The Warrior." We decided that the wonderful character actor Eduard Franz was just the one to play the role of the hundred-year-old Indian. So Franz was cast. About three days before the filming was to begin we learned that Ralph Waite and Will Geer insisted a real Indian be cast in the role. The American Indian Movement became involved and the whole situation became difficult. So auditions were held. Mostly young Indians in their twenties tried out for the role of the old warrior. One man in his sixties came to the auditions and, although his acting experience was limited (he was a film extra), we cast him for the look alone. I was furious. I felt a wonderful script had been sacrificed. The filming was completed, and during it my relationship with the two rebels was very professional but cool. Several months later I returned to direct another episode, the one bringing Ellen back after her stroke. Will was wonderfully supportive during the difficult filming. On the last day, after the final shot was in the can, I hugged Will as I*

thanked him. He looked at me with a twinkle in his eye and said, "Oh, so you've finally forgiven me?" And I, with a twinkle in my eye responded, "Oh, not entirely, Will, not entirely." Those were my last words with Will Geer. He passed away about three months later.

RALPH SENENSKY, DIRECTOR

The Seashore

Air date: 10/20/77; Writer: W. Marion Hargrove; Director: Lawrence Dobkin
John agrees to spruce up the Baldwins' seaside cottage and takes the family along for a much-needed vacation. They find that a young English girl, a college student at William and Mary, has been living in the cottage trying to deal with the death of her father in the war. Meanwhile, Ben agrees to stay home alone, expecting to live the life of a bachelor, until he is interrupted by Corabeth, the Baldwin sisters, and Mary Ellen and Curt.

The Volunteer

Air date: 10/27/77; Writer: Kathleen Hite; Director: Philip Leacock
Erin declines a marriage proposal from G. W. Haines, driving him to join the army. Later he invites Erin to visit him at the army camp. John says no, but later he says yes in spite of his reluctance. Maud Gormley and Ike set up an arrangement for him to sell her paintings in the store. Meanwhile, Jim-Bob and Zeb deal with Rover, their lonely peacock.

Mary Jackson (Emily Baldwin) relaxes at home.

The Grandchild

Air date: 11/03/77 (two-hour episode); Writers: Rod Peterson and Claire Whitaker; Director: Ralph Senensky
Mary Ellen is expecting, and John and Olivia discuss their feelings about being grand-

parents. Cassie, a poor mountain girl, gives birth, with Mary Ellen's help, to a stillborn baby. This event causes great apprehension in Mary Ellen. Eventually she gives birth to John Curtis Willard, but Cassie steals John Curtis. He is returned unharmed. After a fire at the Dew Drop Inn, Jason secretly gets a job playing the piano at a burlesque theater in Charlottesville.

The First Casualty

Air date: 11/10/77; Writer: Andy White; Director: Harry Harris
Yancy Tucker and Sissy are married, and Yancy goes off to war. Dr. Curt Willard is called to active duty to serve in the U.S. Medical Corps. Yancy Tucker returns from the army. He was turned down because of flat feet. George William (G. W.) Haines is killed in a training accident and bequeaths his land to Erin.

> *This was the very moving story of G. W. Haines becoming a casualty due to a training accident. G. W. and Erin had become close. She had actually gone to Camp Lee to visit him, and now he was dead. I remember that we filmed the episode on location, and we shot the scene where Ralph consoles me in a big open field where the grass was a foot tall. The wind kept blowing it and the clouds kept going over, giving a very somber mood to the already somber scene. When I look at the scene today it brings to mind the painting by Andrew Wyeth called* Christina's World.
>
> MARY McDONOUGH, ACTOR (ERIN WALTON)

The Battle of Drucilla's Pond

Air date: 11/17/77; Writers: Rod Peterson and Claire Whitaker; Director: Philip Leacock
Grandpa agrees to permit the army to camp and practice war games at Drucilla's Pond. Olivia paints some quiet scenes from around Walton's Mountain and enters them in a local art show. Grandpa secretly buys them, and after an angry Olivia tells him that she is embarrased, he tells her they are a legacy for the family. Chance gives birth to a calf that Jim-Bob names "Dynamite."

> *Tourists looking for Drucilla's Pond today won't find it. When I was a boy it was located at the foot of the hill past the Baptist church. As the years passed, topsoil washed down and filled it.*

Today only a few cattails and a marsh mark the spot where once we caught bluegill and smallmouth bass.

EARL HAMNER

The Flight

Air date: 12/01/77; Writers: Carole Raschella and Michael Raschella; Director: Ralph Waite

Jim-Bob makes a new friend named Joe Douglas, who tells the family he is on his way to join the air corps. Elizabeth "adopts" Maud Gormley as a substitute grandmother and finds Myrtle the goat at Maud's barn. Myrtle has her baby and Elizabeth names it "Gingerbread." Joe and his sister are actually runaway orphans who are eventually adopted by Sheriff Ep Bridges and his wife, Sarah.

The Children's Carol

Air date: 12/05/77 (two-hour episode); Writer: John McGreevey; Director: Lawrence Dobkin

The Walton family welcomes to the mountain two orphaned English children battle-scarred by the war. The young boy has not spoken since his home was bombed. Ike and Ben conduct a blackout civil defense drill. Mary Ellen rents an apartment near Curt's army base, while Jim-Bob talks to London on his shortwave radio and the children's mother is found. The young boy, Pip, is played by Kami Cotler's brother, Jeff.

> *This is a two-hour, wartime Christmas show that, through two refugee English children, brought new aspects of the war to Walton's Mountain. I cherish this memory because the music director, Alexander (Sandy) Courage, and I collaborated on the carol—lyrics and music. I had my first and only listing with Broadcast Music Incorporated. The carol, alas, proved not to be competition for "Rudolph, the Red-Nosed Reindeer." I am not living off my royalties.*

JOHN MCGREEVEY, WRITER

The Milestone

Air date: 12/08/77; Writer: Kathleen Hite; Director: Philip Leacock

Olivia finds it difficult to cope with minor situations and tells John that she needs to "go home again." She visits her aunt Kate in her hometown of Alberene. Aunt Kate suspects Olivia is going through "the change of life" and asks Olivia to see a doctor. Jim-Bob fakes his mother's signature on a job application and John works on their dream house on the mountain.

The Celebration

Air date: 12/22/77; Writer: Marion Hargrove; Director: Gwen Arner
John discovers that only two payments remain on their house mortgage and the family is almost out of debt. He signs a big contract for three hundred fence posts and the whole family pitches in to get the job done. During the mortgage-burning party, Ike announces that the bank is foreclosing on the store because he owes a large sum on the used refrigerators he bought. John and Olivia agree to co-sign the loan and are back in debt again.

> *I will never forget this episode. It was my first directing job in television, and it was the Walton support team that made it possible. The entire cast welcomed me enthusiastically, and when the filming was finished they threw a party to celebrate. It was also "The Celebration" of my life, and many years and TV shows later, the Walton family of actors was the warmest company I was ever to meet.*
>
> GWEN ARNER, DIRECTOR

The Rumor

Air date: 1/05/78; Writer: Kathleen Hite; Director: Ralph Waite
War feelings run high on the mountain with the arrival of Willy Brimmer and his family, who are searching for work and a place to live. Elizabeth's imagination as a writer races along, and she unknowingly contributes to the growing feeling that the Brimmers are really German spies. Some townspeople are suspicious of their German accents and secretive ways, but John comes to their aid.

Spring Fever

Air date: 1/12/78; Writers: Rod Peterson and Claire Whitaker; Director: Richard Chaffee
Spring brings little joy to Walton's Mountain. Mamie Baldwin's rosebush is dying, and she views that as a sign from her dead

father that this will be her last spring. After considerable objection, Zeb agrees to be the executor of her will. Jim-Bob and Ben have spring fever and end up dating each other's girlfriends, finally coming to blows over their jealousy. Miss Mamie finally comes out of her depression at a Walton picnic, and the boys realize that they have been acting silly.

The Festival

Air date: 1/26/78; Writer: Michael McGreevey; Director: Gwen Arner
Jason and Josh team up to play their music at the upcoming Spring Festival. When Verdie and Harley learn of the plan, they are upset that Josh might not be accepted at the all-white function. Elizabeth and Aimee Godsey experience spring fever.

> *"The Festival" was important to me for several reasons. Not only was it my first job as a writer, but I was writing a story about characters (Verdie Grant, her son, and her husband) that my father had created in earlier episodes. In viewing the finished show, I learned that a great director (in this case Gwen Arner) could make what I had written even better than I had imagined. The episode also generated my most memorable piece of fan mail—an angry letter from a white supremacist who accused me of being a "nigger-lover." I gladly accepted the title.*
>
> MICHAEL MCGREEVEY, WRITER

The Anniversary

Air date: 2/02/78; Writers: Rod Peterson and Claire Whitaker; Director: Walter Alzmann
John and Olivia celebrate their twenty-fifth wedding anniversary. Olivia surprises John with a telephone, and John builds a gazebo for Olivia on the top of the mountain, where the whole family gathers for a picnic. Mary Ellen and Curt are having problems being separated by the army.

> *There was a wonderful chemistry between Ralph Waite and Michael Learned, and we admired the way they portrayed married love. John had always promised to build Olivia a house on the mountain but that dream was never to come true, and so in this story we came up with a compromise: He would build her a*

Ralph Waite and
Michael Learned as
John and Olivia
Walton.

gazebo for their twenty-fifth anniversary. It was a romantic notion
that worked, and we managed to get a lot of family fun into the
episode as well. The ending is notable for having Olivia take her
first sip of champagne.

ROD AND CLAIRE PETERSON, WRITERS

If I had to pick a favorite episode it would probably be this one. It
celebrated a special occasion for John and Olivia, and it gave
Ralph and me the opportunity to play many different facets of our
characters. The entire cast was active in the episode and it was
fun to interact with the whole clan. Olivia was often so strait-
laced that I have to confess, I got a secret pleasure out of the fact
that at the end of the episode she had her first sip of champagne.

MICHAEL LEARNED, ACTOR (OLIVIA WALTON)

The Family Tree

Air date: 2/09/78; Writer: Thomas Hood; Story: Thomas Hood and Joyce Perry; Director: Lawrence Dobkin

Verdie enlists the aid of Jason in her search for her roots and her family history. She runs into many obstacles, but with help from Zeb she is able to make progress. Elizabeth corresponds with a soldier who thinks she is eighteen. The soldier arrives on Walton's Mountain and learns the truth.

> *I was proud of this episode and always felt it was the* Walton *equivalent of* Roots. *I was thrilled to have the chance to work with a wonderful actress and a great lady, Lynn Hamilton, who played Verdie Grant. In the episode, Jason helps Verdie research her ancestry, eventually confronting the wealthy plantation owner whose ancestors had "owned" Verdie's family. This was an episode with much substance. I felt great about the performances as well as about what the episode had to say.*
>
> JON WALMSLEY, ACTOR (JASON WALTON)

The Ordeal

Air date: 2/16/78 (two-hour episode); Writer: Paul West; Director: Lawrence Dobkin

John tells Ben and Jim-Bob to tightly secure a log pile near the mill. They go swimming instead. Meanwhile, Elizabeth climbs up on the log pile to rescue a little bird. The log pile collapses and Elizabeth is injured. Elizabeth is rushed to the hospital where John and Olivia learn that both her legs are broken and she also has nerve damage. Coming home from the hospital, she can only walk with crutches until, one day, Jim-Bob convinces her to walk.

> *Looking back over some of the episodes, I remember that Michael Learned said once that Elizabeth's experiences filming the show were enough to make her quite nuts. Her raccoon died, her horse had to be shot, she was haunted by a poltergeist, her suppressed memory of a man's accidental death resulted in a spate of sleepwalking and she climbed a Ferris wheel in her sleep, she broke both her legs and was unable to walk, her favorite teacher died,*

and she was taken hostage by an angry local man. Quite a full life!

KAMI COTLER, ACTOR (ELIZABETH WALTON)

The Return

Air date: 3/16/78 (two-hour episode); Writer: Kathleen Hite; Director: Harry Harris

Mr. Johnson from the Associated Press assigns John-Boy to write a story about the poor economic situation in the Walton's Mountain area. John-Boy returns home and suggests to his father that they should talk to Mr. Guthrie about reopening the old Guthrie Coal Mine. Mr. Guthrie agrees to open the mine if John assumes the responsibility for repairs. While John and the other men are working inside the mine, there is a cave-in and all the workers are trapped. After a valiant effort, the men are rescued, repairs are eventually made, and the mine provides work until the vein of coal is exhausted.

The Revelation

Air date: 3/23/78; Writers: D. C. Fontana and Richard Fontana; Director: Gwen Arner

John-Boy calls Walton's Mountain with the news that he and Daisy are to be married. They return home to make arrangements for the wedding. Grandpa secretly adds some recipe to the lemonade that Elizabeth plans to sell outside of Ike's store. John-Boy contacts Daisy's mother and learns that Daisy has a three-year-old daughter. Their marriage is canceled when they both realize that their lives are going in different directions. John-Boy agrees to take an assignment as a reporter for *Stars and Stripes* in war-torn Europe.

Grandma Comes Home

Air date: 3/30/78; Writers: Rod Peterson and Claire Whitaker; Director: Ralph Senensky

The family rejoices at the news that Grandma is returning home. While safe in their love, she is overly protected and no longer feels needed. Everyone performs their chores but won't permit Esther to be productive. After reading her diary, Zeb finally explains that he had promised God she could just sit and rock if he spared her life.

From now on, however, she would be treated just like everyone else. This was Ellen Corby's first appearance in the series since her stroke, and this was Will Geer's last episode. He died suddenly during the show's summer hiatus.

Will Geer and Ellen Corby as Zeb and Esther Walton.

> *There was never any question that Ellen Corby would return to work after her stroke. The cast—particularly Will Geer—insisted, and despite partial paralysis and loss of speech, she was game. In this episode we wanted to show how easy it is, out of love and concern, to relegate an elderly or handicapped person to a passive role in life and a feeling of uselessness. We were on hand the day Ellen came back to work, and will never forget watching her make her way laboriously and valiantly across the sound stage to the set and resume her role as Grandma Walton.*
>
> ROD AND CLAIRE PETERSON, WRITERS

> *This was the show where Grandma returns after her stroke. It was also the last episode filmed before the death of Will Geer. It was a very emotional reunion. Even though Ellen's speech was very lim-*

ited, her ability to communicate with one word or a look was truly amazing. In an industry where performers are considered not only replaceable but altogether disposable, Ellen's return to the show was one of the most courageous and commendable decisions I have seen by the producers of any show.

JON WALMSLEY, ACTOR (JASON WALTON)

I watched the filming of this episode with awe—Ellen Corby's performance was a testimony to the strength of the human spirit when Grandma comes home for the first time after her stroke. How ironic that this episode was to be Will Geer's last performance, so unforgettably and endearingly acted.

JOE CONLEY, ACTOR (IKE GODSEY)

What can I say about the courage of Ellen Corby! Ellen could be a trial at times. If she fought it was not for a bigger dressing room or time off or a bigger salary. She just wanted to be able to contribute more to the show. Her scene on the porch with Michael, snapping green beans, when Grandma breaks down because she feels nobody needs her—it was breathtaking to watch and to film.

RALPH SENENSKY, DIRECTOR

Season Seven (1978–1979)

The Empty Nest

Air date: 9/21/78 (two-hour episode); Writers: Rod Peterson and Claire Whitaker; Director: Philip Leacock

Each member of the family finds it difficult to deal with the death of Grandpa. With the death of Flossie Brimmer, Zuleika Dunbar takes over the boarding house. Mary Ellen and Erin find an apartment to share in Charlottesville. Lonely for the family, they move back home. John works hard to land a lumber contract with Matt Sarver. The Waltons visit Grandpa's grave on his birthday and give him individual good-byes.

This episode was most memorable because of its tribute to Grandpa Walton. In the story John Walton is tempted to leave the mountain, but in the end the whole family gathers at his graveside to remember Grandpa and to speak to his memory. John vows that

*he will never move away, and each of the children tells some piece
of news that they know Grandpa would have appreciated. It is a
heartbreaker of an episode, and no moment can ever be so moving
as when Ellen Corby, her speech handicapped by her stroke, says,
"Old Man, you live in our hearts."*

PAUL HAMNER, MODEL FOR BEN WALTON

When I was young I would watch The Waltons *with my brothers
and sister. We would laugh until we cried and argue about silly
things, but we always knew we could depend on each other. The
notion of the love and devotion of family members to each other
often seems undervalued and outdated today. The Waltons
always makes me look at my family and appreciate the love and
laughter.*

BETHAN DICKSON, FAN—MIDDLESEX, ENGLAND

*A tremendously moving show because it was a special episode ded-
icated to the memory of Will Geer. The memorial to Will is held at
Grandpa Walton's gravesite, and each member of the cast pays
tribute to Will, who was such a rich presence on the series and so
universally loved by the cast as well as by the fans.*

DUANE SHELL, FAN—LOS ANGELES, CALIFORNIA

The Calling

Air date: 9/28/78; Writer: Kathleen Hite; Director: Gwen Arner
The Baldwins' cousin, Mary Frances Conover, a young girl who is
preparing to be a nun, provides the unsuspecting Jim-Bob with a
new romantic interest. Ben hires a likable stranger to work in the
mill but later learns that he is an unreliable alcoholic. Mary
Frances tells Jim-Bob the truth and he is heartbroken.

*Thanks to the Hamner family for allowing the events of their lives
to be the basis for this wonderful series.*

EDNA FIELD, FAN—CHESHIRE ENGLAND

The Moonshiner

Air date: 10/12/78; Writer: Jeb Rosebrook; Director: Lawrence Dobkin
A judge finds Boone Walton (Morgan Woodward) guilty of selling
moonshine whiskey. Jason tells the judge that he will be responsible

Morgan Woodward
as Boone Walton.

for Boone and will pay the $100 fine. Jason takes him home, to the chagrin of Olivia. After her mother dies, Daisy Garner comes for a visit to close up her mother's house and to return John-Boy's engagement ring to Olivia. Boone helps the Baldwin sisters with their moonshine when they lose their recipe for the recipe. After paying Jason the $100, Boone disappears into the mountain. He is killed by a truck while crossing the highway carrying two gallons of moonshine.

In this episode I brought back Boone Walton, a character I had introduced in "The Conflict." Morgan Woodward wonderfully reprised his role as the relative whose moonshining ways were severely disapproved of by Grandma and Olivia.

JEB ROSEBROOK, WRITER

The Obsession

Air date: 10/19/78; Writer: Juliet Packer; Director: Gwen Arner
Olivia is concerned with the long hours Mary Ellen is working and studying to pass her nursing test. Mary Ellen begins to take prescription drugs in an attempt to stay awake and give her more time to cram. Cissy, Yancy Tucker's wife, has had enough of the animals in the house and declares that either the animals must go or she will. Curt arrives at Mary Ellen's graduation and announces that he has been transferred to a place called Pearl Harbor.

This was my first writing assignment on The Waltons. *The subplot involves Sissy, who has decided to leave Yancy because she is tired of his keeping all his pets in the house. Since I was a freelance writer, changes sometimes occurred in the script after my final submission. Imagine my surprise when I watched the show on the air and heard Yancy defending the chicken, which liked to roost on his bed. "This here is Earl," says Yancy. "My best friend."*

And Sissy counters, "I'm tired of finding Earl in my scanties!" I want it on record and I want Earl Hamner to know that I did not write those lines of dialogue!

JULIET LAW PACKER, WRITER

All the events of Mary Ellen's teenage years are very dear to me. Perhaps it is because I grew up in those same years that they are so memorable. School years, falling in love and getting married, having brothers and sisters go off to war and then returning, the passing of beloved grandparents, everyday happenings in everyday lives are what life is about.

JUNE ASH, FAN—ODENVILLE, ALABAMA

The Changeling

Air date: 10/26/78; Writer: Robert Pirosh; Director: Lawrence Dobkin
Elizabeth experiences internal conflict as she develops into a teenager. Jason wins an audition for a new love advice program on a local radio program. His radio identity is "Cousin George." Strange things begin to happen around Elizabeth. During an all-night birthday party she comes face-to-face with her fear of the future.

The Portrait

Air date: 11/02/78; Writer: John Dunkel; Director: Ralph Senensky
An artist returns from Paris to his home on the mountain. He asks Erin to pose for him as part of a war memorial mural he is painting. At first she is flattered, but then she becomes afraid of the mysterious painter. Eventually he forces Erin to pose. The family rushes to her aid and takes the painter to his doctor friend for medical help.

The Captive

Air date: 11/09/78; Writer: Ray Cunneff; Director: Ralph Waite
It is time for Elizabeth to learn how to drive, and she asks Jim-Bob to be her teacher. All does not go well and the two siblings argue about her attitude. Corabeth's increasing drinking problem becomes severe, and Elizabeth is forced to drive Corabeth and Aimee home from a dance studio. Corabeth asks John to help her stop drinking.

I cannot pick any one episode above another. Each episode had some element that touched each of us. The whole series reminded me of my own life and it included the sad times as well as the happy times we all experienced.

JUNE LESTER, FAN—SUFFOLK, ENGLAND

The Illusion

Air date: 11/16/78; Writer: John McGreevey; Director: Walter Alzmann
Ike proudly displays his new Military Honor Roll plaque that lists the men from Walton's Mountain in the service. Unfortunately he has divided the names into white and black. Verdie's daughter, Esther, returns to the mountain sad and depressed by her inability to obtain meaningful employment. Erin introduces Esther to J. D. Pickett, who ultimately agrees to hire her as the personnel director for his defense plant. Verdie asks Ike to redo the plaque, eliminating the black/white division.

When Verdie Grant's daughter, Esther, comes to the mountain and has trouble finding work, Erin helps her find a job at J. D. Pickett's plant. Esther was played by that magnificent actress Joan Pringle. I have always been proud that our series portrayed African Americans in non-stereotypical roles.

MARY MCDONOUGH, ACTOR (ERIN WALTON)

The Beau

Air date: 11/23/78; Writers: D. C. Fontana and Richard Fontana; Director: Gwen Arner
Marcus Dane, a former suitor, drops in for a visit with Grandma. The family is taken aback a bit, especially Elizabeth, who views the situation as disrespectful to the memory of Grandpa. After being told by Ike that there is a gasoline shortage, Jim-Bob convinces Yancy to make fuel in his still instead of moonshine, but the government is not interested. Grandma tells Marcus that she cannot have a romantic relationship with him because her heart still belongs to Zeb.

The Day of Infamy

Air date: 12/07/78; Writer: Paul Savage; Director: Harry Harris
Mary Ellen prepares to go to Hawaii to be with Curt. John and
Olivia plan an early Christmas so that Mary Ellen and John Curtis
can be part of the celebration. News of Pearl Harbor arrives, and
the scattered family returns home to comfort each other. The next
day Verdie arrives with news that Jodie was wounded in the
attack. Jim-Bob brings a telegram saying that Curt was killed.

> *This was my favorite episode. Mary Ellen was so full of hope and
> happiness for her family being reunited in Hawaii. It was a big
> step for her leaving the mountain and traveling with her baby
> across the ocean, but she looked forward to being with her hus-
> band, who was serving in the army there. Then came the attack
> on Pearl Harbor and soon the notification that her husband was
> dead. What truly touched my heart was how supportive her fam-
> ily was to her and how she gained her strength from their love and
> embrace. They gave her the courage to go on. It's how a family
> should be.*
>
> MRS. SAM HARRIS, FAN—FREDERICKSBURG, VIRGINIA

The Yearning

Air date: 12/14/78; Writer: Juliet Packer; Director: Nell Cox
Andrew March, the new minister, stays with the Waltons while a
skunk is being removed from the parsonage. Elizabeth is smitten
with the new minister. While Erin helps the Baldwin sisters write
their memoirs, they come across a letter written by Ashley
Longworth. In anger, Miss Emily removes her father's portrait from
the mantle and discovers the letter. They finally find a ring left by
Ashley more than forty years ago.

> *This show is all about unrequited love. Not only thirteen-year-old
> Elizabeth's crush on the new minister, but "shattering" new infor-
> mation is discovered about Miss Emily's long-lost beau, Ashley
> Longworth. I wanted to write about Elizabeth's first love because I
> had so many cases of puppy love when I was growing up it was
> like living in a kennel. When the minister has to tell Elizabeth that
> he can't return her romantic feelings, Elizabeth is luckier than
> many girls because her parents are there for her. They never dis-*

miss her feelings as a teenage crush. They acknowledge the very real pain she is feeling.

JULIET LAW PACKER, WRITER

The Boosters

Air date: 12/28/78; Writer: Robert Pirosh; Director: Harry Harris
Ben and Ike decide to open an auto court to make lots of money. John declines to participate because he thinks there would be no customers after the war. Ben, however, proceeds with the plan and convinces the townspeople to join the venture. Yancy Tucker enrolls in a mail-order barbering class but has a hard time finding volunteers to have their hair cut.

The Conscience

Air date: 1/04/79; Writer: Michael McGreevey; Director: Gwen Arner
Jason, unlike his brothers, has reservations about joining the military. He is considering becoming a conscientious objector. A fight ensues at the Dew Drop Inn between Jason and some boys who believe Jason is a coward. After a night of reflection on the mountain, Jason joins the army. Jim-Bob gets a military tattoo, much to the consternation of Olivia.

> *"The Conscience" was the episode that was most personal to me. Having experienced my own crisis of conscience while facing the draft during the Vietnam War, it was very cathartic for me to write about Jason's struggle with whether or not he could kill another human being in the heat of battle. I learned a lot about myself and my beliefs while writing "The Conscience."*

MICHAEL McGREEVEY, WRITER

The Obstacle

Air date: 1/11/79; Writer: Curtis Dwight; Director: William Bushnell Jr.
The family receives a letter from John-Boy asking them to check up on his friend, Mike Paxton, who is confined to a wheelchair and has not responded to John-Boy's letters. Mary Ellen visits Mike and convinces him to return with her to Walton's Mountain. The family helps Mike to come out of his shell and get a job at the Pickett defense plant.

The Parting

Air date: 1/18/79; Writer: Kathleen Hite;
Director: Harry Harris
Olivia is concerned that John is working too much and urges him to see a
doctor. While on a resting trip to
Virginia Beach, Olivia experiences hot
spells and they stop in Alberene
where Olivia visits with Aunt Kate's
Doctor Caldwell. After returning
home, they receive a surprise visit
from Aunt Kate with bad news. Olivia
is diagnosed with tuberculosis and
must go to a sanatorium.

The Burden

Air date: 1/25/79; Writer: E. F.
Wallengren; Director: Harry Harris
Jim-Bob is working under his car
when the jack slips and he is pinned

David Harper as Jim-
Bob Walton.

under the vehicle. Somehow he is not injured and sees this as a
sign from God. Jim-Bob visits with Reverend Bradshaw, who later
announces to the congregation that Jim-Bob wants to become a
minister. Jim-Bob tells his father that he feels responsible for all
the family's woes. John reminds him not to place himself at the
center of life.

> *After being repeatedly rebuffed by my mom and stepdad, who*
> *were producer and story editor for several seasons of* The
> Waltons, *I called Earl, who graciously agreed to go to lunch with*
> *me, unaware that he was about to be ambushed. I pitched him the*
> *story of "The Burden" and Jim-Bob's near brush with religion. He*
> *bought it on the spot, leaving me with the painful ordeal of*
> *explaining to my parents that I had pulled the oldest trick in the*
> *Hollywood book—I had engaged in non-consensual nepotism. I*
> *don't know if my parents ever forgave me, even though the episode*

Ike and Corabeth Godsey, played by Joe
Conley and Ronnie Claire Edwards.

Jonathan Frakes
(Ashley Longworth Jr.).

was nominated for a Writer's Guild Award and I was shortly thereafter placed on the Waltons *writing staff.*

ERNIE WALLENGREN, WRITER

The Pin-Up

Air date: 2/08/79; Writer: Juliet Packer; Director: Larry Stewart
Erin finds herself embroiled in a family controversy when Ben enters her photograph in a newspaper contest and wins first place. John is furious when he learns that her picture is posted all over Camp Lee and has become the "official" pin-up of the soldiers. Meanwhile, Mary Ellen frets over her role as a protective mother to John Curtis and eventually learns that a mother can only do so much.

> *This episode had parallel stories. We see Mary Ellen clutching too tightly to John Curtis, while John, meanwhile, is overly protective of Erin. By the end of the episode both have loosened their grip. This episode was filmed in 1978, and Mary Beth McDonough had blossomed from a little girl into a beautiful young woman. She becomes a "pin-up" girl when a leggy picture of her dressed in shorts is on the cover of the local newspaper. John is scandalized. So is Corabeth! It was especially fun coming up with appellations for the pin-up girl. First we learn she is known as the "Jefferson County Cutie." Then she becomes the "Sweetheart of Camp Lee." I felt quite envious of Erin.*
>
> JULIET LAW PACKER, WRITER

The Attack

Air date: 2/15/79; Writer: E. F. Wallengren; Director: Harry Harris
Ike has a heart attack, and Corabeth insists that they sell the store and Ike retire. Elizabeth and the other Walton children pitch in and keep the store running. Ben and Jim-Bob go into the molasses business but find the going is rough and not very profitable. Two businessmen look over the store but Ike can't push himself to sell.

> *As an actor I have never had to die on camera, but in this episode I was to come close as Ike beats the grim reaper. This was a lovely script.*
>
> JOE CONLEY, ACTOR (IKE GODSEY)

The Legacy

Air date: 2/22/79; Teleplay: William Parker; Story: Michael Learned; Director: Gwen Arner

The Baldwin sisters enlist Erin in the writing of their memoirs. Ashley Longworth Jr. appears on the mountain and captures Miss Emily Baldwin's heart, but Ashley Jr. only has eyes for Erin. Ashley Jr. gives Miss Emily a letter from his dead father. Miss Emily catches Ashley Jr. kissing Erin under the same tree Ashley Sr. had kissed her.

Ashley Longworth had been a character Miss Emily talked about incessantly. She would stop you at Ike's store and tell you about the time Ashley Longworth kissed her in October in a shower of golden leaves. Our family halfway believed that Ashley Longworth was somebody Miss Emily had made up until one day Ashley Longworth's son turned up. He wasn't a dream, but the actor, Jonathan Frakes, was a dreamboat. Yes, the script called for another kissing scene, but this time it was no problem at all!

MARY MCDONOUGH, ACTOR (ERIN WALTON)

I had just come out from New York where I had been doing soap and had little experience with television in Hollywood. To my great good luck I was cast as Ashley Longworth Jr., the son of the University of Virginia student who had so boldly kissed Miss Emily Baldwin "in a shower of golden leaves"—an act so vile it caused her father, the judge, to ask him to leave town! At any rate, I was welcomed by the Walton cast and treated with genuine warmth and respect. I was honored by a decision that had to be made while I was in one episode. It was after Will Geer's death, and nobody had ever sat in his place at the table. It was decided that sufficient time had passed and that my character was a nice enough guy that I was allowed to sit there. It is still an honor. I also remember my first day on the set I went into the makeup trailer. Kami Cotler was in the next chair, She was every bit of seven years old, and while she was being made up she was reading the Wall Street Journal *and checking her stock portfolio!*

JONATHAN FRAKES, ACTOR (ASHLEY LONGWORTH JR.)

The Outsider

Air date: 3/01/79; Writer: Robert Pirosh; Director: Philip Leacock
Ben surprises the family when he shows up in the middle of the night with Cindy, his new bride. The newlyweds set up house-keeping in the shed. The next day Cindy and Ben have their first of many disagreements over money and their relationship. Meanwhile, Ike purchases a fountain at Doe Hill and surprises Corabeth. Cindy announces she is leaving until Grandma shows her how to use a broom on Ben like she did on Grandpa.

The Torch

Air date: 3/08/79; Writer: Rod Peterson; Director: David Wheeler
Jason is concerned for his job as piano player when he learns that the Dew Drop Inn has been sold. The new owner hires him and also hires John to do some remodeling. It seems the new owner, Callie May Jordan, is John's old friend and classmate. She obvi-ously has "eyes" for John, and the children try to protect their father from her attention. With Callie May's help, Ike and the girls turn Godsey Hall into a canteen for the soldiers of Camp Rockfish.

The Tailspin

Air date: 3/15/79; Writer: Claire Whitaker; Director: Walter Alzmann
Jim-Bob is saddened and disgruntled when he fails an eye exam and realizes that he cannot become a pilot in the army air corps. He announces that he is dropping out of school and joining the army. Meanwhile, Mary Ellen discovers that she is attracted to Chuck Turner, one of Curt's old childhood friends. With Corabeth's help and summer school, Jim-Bob stays in school.

> *I had always been drawn to the character of Jim-Bob, who was played with such great sensitivity by David Harper, and I wanted to provide him with a vehicle of his own. In trying to come up with a plot I asked myself what would rattle his world, and it came to me that the shattering of his life's dream—to fly—would provide conflict. David did some fine work and of course, it being* The Waltons *I was able to devise a happy ending. The scene in the tree house between Jim-Bob and his father was inspired by my son*

Eric, who always took to the avocado tree in our patio when he was upset. It was my favorite scene in the show.

ROD AND CLAIRE PETERSON, WRITERS

Founder's Day

Air date: 3/22/79; Writer: Kathleen Hite; Director: Ralph Waite
As a final requirement for graduation, Jason must write an original musical score. He and his professor differ on what constitutes good music. Jason is required to write in the classical manner, but he wants to compose something more contemporary. The Baldwin sisters, Corabeth, and Mary Ellen organize "Founder's Day" in celebration of their community. Jason composes "Appalachian Portrait" and plays it during the festivities. His professor is in the audience and agrees that Jason's work is excellent. Earl Hamner presents a poignant narrative on the Blue Ridge and the Walton family.

"The Walton Theme" is a prelude for me to every episode and I never skip over it. The first time I went to visit the museum I had the music playing on a tape in my car. I made sure the windows were rolled down and I played it loud so everyone would know I was a fan on her way to Walton's Mountain.

SHARON HOLMES, FAN

Music played an important role in every episode but it was especially important in this one. The theme music was the work of the distinguished composer Jerry Goldsmith. The main title was unusual. Part of Jerry's genius is his search for an unusual sound to integrate into his scores. In this theme he employed a special kind of guitar and of course that famous trumpet solo. I assisted Jerry for the first two years, and in the third year he got busy in movies and turned the job of composer over to me. Jerry set the tone for the entire series. He was doing a kind of sophisticated Flatt and Scruggs, and I was looking to go back to the English folk-song type of music. I think we achieved something somewhere in between. In any kind of film what you do is fill up the lack of sound and substantiate the emotion of the scene. Generally I worked with a small orchestra, a little chamber orchestra, actually. It was a grand, grand pleasure to do the show. I had scored a lot of crime shows before, so to compose music for this nice show about nice people was heaven-sent.

ALEXANDER (SANDY) COURAGE, COMPOSER

There are aristocrats and horse thieves in all of our family trees. Perhaps that is why I have a particular fondness for this episode. Even the shadow cast by a Walton ancestor's controversial diary entry is embraced and brought to light for the truth it brings forth. Kith and kin are not abandoned or denied. Family is family, after all. Each time I view this episode I find myself pulling out my old photo album, cracked and worn with years, and I trace the faces of those dear folks from long ago. From straight shoulders and sharp profiles they have carried my family history to me. The pioneers and poets, farmers and steel mill workers, the immigrants leaving countrymen and homeland for the shores of America; they are mine. Moonshiners and coal miners, they are my own people, gone before me yet rising up within me. "Founders Day" gives me cause to celebrate the human soil through which I've come.

JAMIE MOREWOOD ANDERSON, FAN—CEDAR CREST, NEW MEXICO

Season Eight (1979–1980)

The Home Front

Air date: 9/20/79 (two-hour episode); Writers: Rod Peterson and Claire Whitaker; Director: Harry Harris
Sheriff Bridges informs John that a local draftee has run away from the army. As head of the local draft board, John finds the boy and talks him into going back. The young soldier is killed, and the boy's father threatens John with revenge. The family receives a dreaded telegram informing them that John-Boy is missing in action.

The Kinfolk

Air date: 9/27/79; Writer: E. F. Wallengren; Director: Philip Leacock
Cousin Rose Burton arrives on the mountain with her two undisciplined grandchildren, Serena and Jeffrey. She eventually admits that her son had abused his children and she desperately needs sanctuary for them. As the local air warden, Ike receives and

installs a siren big enough for a major city.

I had watched The Waltons *even before I joined the cast, and it seemed that people were constantly arriving there on foot, by car, truck, motorcycle, so when they cast me I wondered how I would arrive. It turned out my character, Aunt Rose, and my two grandchildren, Serena and Jeffrey, arrived by bus. We were latecomers to the family, but they received us literally "with open arms."*

PEGGY REA, ACTOR (ROSE BURTON)

Earl Hamner and Peggy Rea (Rose Burton).

The Diploma

Air date: 10/04/79; Writer: Kathleen Hite; Director: Gwen Arner
The county nurse asks Mary Ellen to substitute for her while she is away serving in the army nursing corps. Meanwhile, John tries to prove to the army that he really did graduate from high school even though he can't find his diploma. Olivia discovers that the diplomas for the boys who served in WWI were never issued. John takes a makeup test.

The Innocents

Air date: 10/11/79; Writer: Juliet Packer; Director: Gwen Arner
After observing conditions at the J. D. Pickett Plant, Olivia decides that the mountain needs a day nursery for the children of the plant workers. J. D. opposes her plans but finally agrees to let her use the bar during the day when it is empty. Ike asks Rose to teach him to dance as a surprise for his fifth wedding anniversary, but Corabeth thinks he has a girlfriend.

I loved this story. I'm no dancer, but I had to learn to tango. It sure tested my talents (and I am sure the director's as well). The script was delightful.

JOE CONLEY, ACTOR (IKE GODSEY)

Michael Learned was very conscious that her character was seen as a role model by many women in the audience, so we took pains to make sure that her role was not a stereotype. As Olivia's contribution to the war effort she starts a daycare center for J. D. Pickett's employees. Once she realizes it is too dangerous to have the children around the mill equipment she storms J. D.'s plant and stages a sit-in with her family and the workers' children. When I first watched the episode and saw Olivia go toe-to-toe with J. D., it was even stronger than I had envisioned. I thought, I'd never want to mess with a woman like Olivia Walton! The subplot was fun to write. Corabeth bemoans Ike's seeming disinterest in their "affaire d'amour." Elizabeth and Aimee decide Ike needs to learn to dance and secretly set up lessons with Rose, once known as the "Belle of the Blue Moon Ballroom." Corabeth smells cheap perfume on Ike's clothes and suspects the worst. But all ends happily when Corabeth is surprised with a candlelight dinner. And when Ike leads her in a tango it is a rare and sweet romantic moment for these two.

JULIET LAW PACKER, WRITER

The Starlet

Air date: 10/18/79; Writers: D. C. Fontana and Richard Fontana; Director: Philip Leacock

At Jason's insistence, several soldiers accept the hospitality of the Baldwin sisters. The Pickett defense plant becomes a film set for a wartime documentary. In return for Erin's help, the director convinces her that she has what it takes to be a movie star.

Another kissing scene! This time with an older man! A Hollywood producer of all people! Looking back it seems I kissed and cried a lot!

MARY MCDONOUGH, ACTOR (ERIN WALTON)

The Journal

Air date: 10/25/79; Writer: Robert Pirosh; Director: Philip Leacock
John and Olivia learn that John-Boy's plane was shot down over Belgium. A representative from his publisher visits the mountain to seek permission to print the new book that John-Boy wrote before he became missing in action. Reckless, the family dog, becomes ill and dies.

The Lost Sheep

Air date: 11/01/79; Writer: E. F. Wallengren; Director: Walter Alzmann
Ashley Longworth Jr., now in the military, returns to Walton's Mountain to ask Erin to be his bride. She accepts but develops concerns when he confesses that he has lost his faith in God. Elizabeth and Serena work out their privacy problems.

The Violated

Air date: 11/08/79; Writer: Robert Pirosh; Director: Walter Alzmann
John and Olivia visit the Red Cross for an update on John-Boy. At the request of Mrs. Denman of the Red Cross, Olivia searches for a soldier's wife who won't answer his letters. The girl has been raped and is too embarrassed to tell her husband. Mrs. Denman visits the mountain and tells the family that John-Boy has been found and will be transferred to a hospital outside Washington, D.C.

The Waiting

Air date: 11/22/79; Writer: Kathleen Hite; Director: Philip Leacock
John and Olivia travel to the hospital to visit John-Boy, who is in a coma. John returns home, but Olivia stays to be near John-Boy and agrees to share an apartment with Mrs. Denman. Meanwhile, Rose plans a big Thanksgiving feast. John returns to the hospital to be with Olivia, and John-Boy moves his arm, indicating that he is improving.

The Silver Wings

Air date: 11/29/79; Writer: Michael McGreevey; Director: Stan Latham
While Jim-Bob acts as a mailman for Ike, he meets Mrs. Betsy Randolph, who becomes the object of his affection. It was never her intention to be involved with him and she innocently hurts his

feelings. She receives word that her husband was killed, and she leaves the mountain. Serena goes on a night hike, gets lost, and is rescued by John.

> *"The Silver Wings" contains a scene that I think is one of the funniest things I have ever written. Jim-Bob has a crush on this older woman and is trying to impress her while they work in her garden. Attempting to make conversation, Jim-Bob begins talking about manure and can't stop himself. He goes on and on about manure, even though he knows that it's not a very romantic subject matter. I remember laughing out loud when I wrote the scene and I laughed even louder when I saw the finished episode.*
>
> MICHAEL MCGREEVEY, WRITER

The Wager

Air date: 12/13/79; Teleplay: E. F. Wallengren; Story: Claylene Jones; Director: Gwen Arner

The Annual Run and Ride Race is coming up, and Mary Ellen and Erin are challenged by two men to enter. Elizabeth is drafted as their coach and works them hard. Although they do not win the race, they do win their bet with the men. Jeffrey dreams of meeting his favorite female movie star, and thanks to Jason his wish comes true.

> *"The Wager" was a story I developed from a newspaper article regarding "Ride and Tie Races " (horseback/foot races run in a relay fashion). The episode, set in World War II, pitted Mary Ellen and Erin against two town bullies, and of course, Mary Ellen and Erin won! I think this story line gave the audience a glimpse of how women were starting to evolve and would find their place in the world outside of the home after the war. A small taste of women's lib in 1944.*
>
> CLAYLENE JONES, WRITER/PRODUCER

> *This was probably the episode I had the most fun filming because I got to spend all day riding horses, one of my great loves in life. I always thought I would love to work on action-adventure projects, and this episode gave me a taste of it.*
>
> JUDY NORTON, ACTOR (MARY ELLEN WALTON)

The Spirit

Air date: 12/20/79; Writer: Kathleen Hite; Director: Herbert Hirschmann
It's Christmastime and strange things are happening on the mountain. Food and clothing are missing and the Baldwin sisters feed a stranger. This stranger is befriended by Jeffrey, who invites him to share Christmas Eve with the family. It turns out that he is half German and half American. He has escaped from a German POW camp in North Carolina. Remembering that a German boat rescued John-Boy after being shot down, the family asks him in on Christmas Eve.

The Fastidious Wife

Air date: 12/27/79; Writer: Loraine Despress; Director: Gwen Arner
Cindy wonders if she is being a good wife and Corabeth gives her a book, *The Fastidious Wife,* which describes how to be the perfect wife. Jeffrey does not realize that "Harold," the stray cat he brings home, is ready to give birth to kittens. The children give away all but one, which they keep.

> *Looking back over some of the episodes I did made me remember what a defining experience the series was in my life. My first memories were of auditioning for the role. I wanted it so badly. While I was in the waiting room I looked around at the other candidates for the role and asked myself: Am I too blonde? Too short? Not pretty enough? Evidently I wasn't any of these things because I got the job! Working on the first episode was wild! Everyone checked me out, especially the girls and Eric Scott. However, Eric and I had magic together and working with each other was a ball! The girls eventually decided I was all right, and we have all been in each other's weddings and other celebrations and have remained cherished friends.*
>
> LESLIE WINSTON, ACTOR (CINDY WALTON)

The Unthinkable

Air date: 1/03/80; Writer: Dan Ullman; Director: Ralph Waite
Jason brings home Ted Lupinsky, a Jewish recruit from his company, who tells the family about the killing of his grandfather in a Polish concentration camp. John tries to verify the existence of

Leslie Winston as
Cindy Walton.

Tony Becker as
Drew Cutler.

such camps but is told they are just rumors. Ted and the family have a picnic at Grandpa's grave where Ted says a prayer for both grandfathers.

The Idol

Air date: 1/10/80; Writer: Juliet Packer; Director: Gwen Arner
Elizabeth becomes attached to the new teacher, Hazel Lamphere, and she is deeply troubled when she learns that Hazel has a terminal brain tumor. Corabeth is outraged when she learns that Hazel is planning a class on childbirth. Ben and Cindy have a baby girl, whom Cindy names Virginia.

> *I am especially fond of this episode because it gave me an opportunity to express my own private passions and beliefs. It's about censorship, personal integrity, taking chances, but mostly it's about friendship. Elizabeth finds a true mentor in the exuberant young woman Hazel, the new teacher. Corabeth takes an immediate dislike to Hazel, who removes Corabeth's insipid portrait of Cupid and replaces it with something imaginative and modern. Quelle horreur! Hazel was the kind of young woman I wanted to be—a kind of Auntie Mame, full of zest, who saw life as an adventure. When Elizabeth warns Hazel that Corabeth is gunning for her, Hazel says: "In life there are always going to be dragons around us. And when a dragon, even a small one, starts breathing fire then we've got to stop it. Sometimes we get a little burned when we try." Later, when Elizabeth learns Hazel is dying, she feels betrayed, as we all do when faced with loss. But Jason and John help Elizabeth see that her friendship will endure beyond the grave, that friends support each other during the bad times, and that we must use the time we have on this earth to show our love. It was a special honor to get to tell this story.*
>
> JULIET LAW PACKER, WRITER

The Prodigals

Air date: 1/17/80; Writer: Robert Pirosh; Director: Stan Latham
Jeffrey and Josh break into Ike's store to steal money to replace a tool for John. Their efforts go badly and they are both punished for their actions. After discussing his plans with John-Boy, Ben decides to enlist in the navy Seabees.

The Remembrance

Air date: 1/24/80; Writer: Marion Hargrove; Director: Herbert Hirschmann

Jason meets Sgt. Toni Hazelton and, after some early bickering, they become attracted to each other. Elderly Cousin Zadoc visits with the family, and during a picnic he bequeaths his farm to Boatwright University and his fiddle to Jason.

The Inspiration

Air date: 1/31/80; Writer: E. F. Wallengren; Director: Ralph Waite

Mamie Baldwin discovers she has cataracts and she needs an operation. She refuses because her father, the judge, died on the operating table. John takes Grandma to the Baldwin home where she convinces Miss Mamie to accept any help that is available.

> *This was the first episode in which I was to play the role of Drew Cutler, but I will remember it all my life. I especially remember walking home with Elizabeth and our first kiss. At first as an actor I thought,* This is a very tight-knit group. They'll never let me in. *But it only took a few episodes until I felt not just a part of the group, but a member of the family.*
>
> Tony Becker, Actor (Drew Cutler)

The Last Straw

Air date: 2/07/80; Writer: William Parker; Director: Harry Harris

John is overwhelmed with work orders, his helper wrecks the truck, his saw burns up, and Jim-Bob breaks his arm. He decides enough is enough and he just "quits." Jeffrey builds a soapbox car, hoping to enter the National Soapbox Derby. He is sponsored by Godsey's store, but Ike finds out that the derby is postponed until after the war. John decides to work again and with the help of his friends gets the mill ready to begin production.

The Traveling Man

Air date: 2/14/80; Writer: Kathleen Hite; Director: Herbert Hirschmann

While shopping at Ike's store, Rose sees Stanley Perkins, her old dancing partner from Baltimore. They socialize and rekindle their previous romance and plan for marriage. Rose learns that Stanley

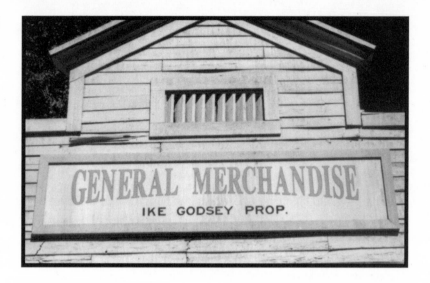

Ike Godsey's General
Merchandise.

has been offered his dream job in California and backs out of the
wedding. Jim-Bob has trouble with Jeffrey's dog being a pest.

> *This was a fun episode because it introduced Stanley Perkins,
> played by Bill Schallert. Our characters were friends from the
> "Blue Moon Ballroom," where we had been dance partners. We
> found each other again at Ike's store, and to show that our hearts
> were still in the right place we did a few "dips" there in the store.*
>
> PEGGY REA, ACTOR (ROSE BURTON)

The Furlough

Air date: 2/21/80; Writer: Juliet Packer; Director: Harry Harris
John-Boy is haunted by his lack of memory concerning the
shooting down of his plane and the death of his close friend,
Stewart. He keeps remembering a name, and it is not until Jim-
Bob shows him a model airplane that it all comes together. Ike
ignores a draft notice from the army and is arrested by the FBI
for draft evasion.

> *In this episode Ike ignores a letter from the draft board and is
> arrested for draft dodging. It was silly and nutty and funny and
> delightfully written—right out of Laurel and Hardy.*
>
> JOE CONLEY, ACTOR (IKE GODSEY)

John-Boy is troubled because he can't remember what happened after he was shot down off the coast of England. He is especially haunted because he doesn't know if the copilot, his closest buddy, survived. When the memories do surface he realizes his friend did die, and John-Boy can begin to grieve. I named the copilot after the man I was in love with at that time. As irony would have it, he shot me down about the time this episode aired. Luckily I survived, but I think there's a lesson there somewhere.

JULIET LAW PACKER, WRITER

The Medal

Air date: 2/28/80; Writer: Rod Peterson; Director: Walter Alzmann
Mary Ellen witnesses a fight between some town bullies and Sgt. Eddie Ramirez, who has come to give her a medal won by Curtis for his bravery at Pearl Harbor. Corabeth meets an old beau who tries to pressure her into a romantic liaison.

The Valedictorian

Air date: 3/13/80; Writer: Claire Whitaker; Director: Harry Harris
Jim-Bob learns that he has been designated as the class valedictorian. He is reluctant to accept the honor until Elizabeth points out that it is his duty. Erin is heartbroken after she learns that Ashley Longworth Jr. has married in London. Walking together, the Walton boys leave for the war.

A Decade of the Waltons

Air date: 5/22/80 (two-hour episode); Writer: Earl Hamner; Directors: Harry Harris and Philip Leacock
It is Grandma's birthday and the family is preparing a photograph album as her present. The first eight seasons of the series are visited through flashbacks. Earl Hamner provides narration throughout, and members of his family in Schuyler, Virginia, are introduced to their corresponding cast members.

This was a very special show. It was the first time we as actors got to speak as our real selves and to ad-lib rather than do scripted speeches. We also got to meet and talk face-to-face with the real-life characters we were portraying. I remember it was the first time I met Audrey, the sister I represented, and I always remember how pretty she was and how glad I was to finally meet her and see what a nice person she was.

MARY McDONOUGH, ACTOR (ERIN WALTON)

Season Nine (1980–1981)

The Outrage

Air date: 11/20/80 (two-hour episode); Writers: Rod Peterson and Claire Whitaker; Director: Philip Leacock

Harley Foster, Verdie's husband, is accused of being an escaped murderer. Harley admits to the crime but says it was self-defense. John drives to Georgia in hopes of asking President Roosevelt for a pardon for Harley. President Roosevelt dies and his body is taken by train to Washington. Meanwhile, Ike and Corabeth struggle to define her role in their marriage.

The Pledge

Air date: 12/04/80; Writer: Kathleen Hite; Director: Lawrence Dobkin

A young mountain boy collapses in front of Mary Ellen and dies. She feels her nurse's training is not adequate for the needs of the community, and she decides to go to medical school and become a doctor. The Baldwin sisters send Jason some recipe, and Corabeth makes a birthday cake for a young soldier stationed nearby.

The Triumph

Air date: 12/18/80; Writer: Robert Pirosh; Director: Philip Leacock

Jason and his squad come under sniper fire just as they learn Germany has surrendered. Ike and Corabeth are caught selling food to the Baldwins without the required ration tickets. When they return from their hearing, they discover the store has been robbed. They decide to close the store but their friends convince them otherwise.

The Premonition

Air date: 12/25/80; Writer: E. F. Wallengren; Director: Bernard McEveety

Cindy has a premonition about Ben and receives a telegram telling her that he has become a prisoner of war. She receives a letter that Ben had mailed weeks earlier in which he describes his dream that she would meet him as his ship pulls into the dock. Meanwhile, John-Boy falls in love with a French girl who asks him to write an article about unexploded mines.

> *Every episode has been special to me. Each embodies the spirit of a warm, close, loving family who has been an example to all who came to love the series. The way each particular family member learns one of life's lessons is a guideline for all to learn from.*
>
> VICKI ELDER, FAN—GLOUCESTERSHIRE, ENGLAND

Ike Godsey's store re-created at the museum.

The Pursuit

Air date: 1/01/81; Writer: Michael McGreevey; Director: Philip Leacock
Kathy, a girl that Jim-Bob has been dating, comes to the mountain to tell him that she is pregnant with his baby. Mary Ellen is suspicious and talks to her father, who in turn talks to Kathy and Jim-Bob about the importance of truth in marriage. Kathy recants and admits she lied. Ben, still a prisoner of war in the Pacific, flies a homemade American flag.

The Last Ten Days

Air date: 1/08/81; Writer: Marion Hargrove; Director: Bernard McEveety
Ben and a fellow prisoner are turned over to American forces. He phones home to Cindy and tells the family he is all right. The war ends while Jason is on leave and he decides to seriously court Toni.

The Move

Air date: 1/15/81; Writer: Kathleen Hite; Director: Harvey S. Laidman
Ben returns from the war and tells his father that he plans to go to college and study engineering. John, depending on Ben's help, is very disappointed and tells the family that he will sell the mill because he must take Olivia to a sanatorium in Arizona. Cindy's father, Colonel Henry Brunson, visits the mountain.

> *One of the pleasures of acting in this episode was the script by Kathleen Hite. Many years ago when I worked on Gunsmoke, Kathleen was a junior writer on the show along with John Meston and Madelyn Pugh. Madelyn, along with her writing partner, Bob Carroll, became the esteemed writers of The Lucy Show. I left Gunsmoke to do a play at the Nixon Theater in Pittsburgh, and on opening night I received two dozen red roses and a Break a Leg message. It had been sent by my Gunsmoke friends Madelyn, John, and Kathleen. Kathleen wrote many wonderful scripts for The Waltons, and whenever I saw her name on a script it was an assurance that it would be original and witty and interesting.*
>
> PEGGY REA, ACTOR (ROSE BURTON)

The Whirlwind

Air date: 1/22/81; Writer: Claire Whitaker; Director: Nell Cox
Jim-Bob thumbs a ride from a passing motorist. The car's brakes fail and the car flips over. Mary Ellen and Jason come to the rescue. The driver is Arlington Jones, who goes by the nickname "Jonesy." He quickly falls in love with Mary Ellen and they talk of marriage, but word comes that Curt might not be dead and may be living in Florida. Jason buys the Dew Drop Inn.

The Tempest

Air date: 2/05/81; Writer: E. F. Wallengren; Director: Gabrielle Beaumont
Mary Ellen travels to Florida, and Curt is indeed alive. He treats her poorly, however, and she comes to realize that she has no future with him. Jonesy goes to work for J. D. Pickett, who has fired Erin. Jonesy intercedes for Erin and she gets her job back. Mary Ellen returns home and continues her relationship with Jonesy.

> *In this episode I am working for J. D. Pickett, played by Lewis Arquette, son of Cliff Arquette and father of Patricia, David, and Rosanna. Talent runs in that family!*
>
> MARY MCDONOUGH, ACTOR (ERIN WALTON)

The Carousel

Air date: 2/12/81; Writer: Robert Pirosh; Director: Herbert Hirschmann
Cindy's father dies in an automobile accident and Ben and Cindy go to Washington, D.C. to take care of her father's affairs. Among her father's papers she comes across a document indicating that she was adopted. She and Ben set out to find her natural mother. While his parents are away, Drew stays with the Waltons but doesn't seem to have much time for Elizabeth.

The Hot Rod

Air date: 2/19/81; Writer: Scott Hamner; Director: Bob Sweeney
The Baldwin sisters are forced by the government to dismantle their recipe machine but accidentally discover the judge's secret room, which contains an older still. Jim-Bob and Jody Foster decide to settle down after the war and team up to open a garage.

I wanted to write a story about race that was not about a conflict between blacks and whites. In "The Hot Rod," Jim-Bob and Jody's friendship is the core of the story, but the conflict arrives when they get into trouble with the law for speeding. Instead of emphasizing their differences, their similarities are stressed and their friendship is never an issue. By veering away from racial issues, the idea was to broaden the presence of black characters by incorporating them into stories that were not race-related.

SCOTT HAMNER, WRITER

The Gold Watch

Air date: 2/26/81; Writer: Juliet Packer; Director: Walt Gilmore
Stanley Perkins returns to Walton's Mountain and tells Rose that he has retired as a salesman and has received a gold watch as a retirement present. Rose discovers that he has suffered a nervous breakdown. Jason, trying to improve business, hires a country singer at the Dew Drop Inn but is forced to fire him when he pays too much attention to his girlfriend, Toni. Rose gives Stanley a gold watch and convinces him that he is not a failure.

I wanted this episode to have a sense of mystery. Rose's longtime dance partner, the traveling man Stanley Perkins, unexpectedly shows up. At first we don't know why he's unkempt, secretive, and anxious. Soon we learn he has been in a hospital, but not why. As the layers unfold we discover he had suffered a mental breakdown after being fired from his job. Stanley, like most people, has no idea how much value and support he brings to others. What I find moving about this story is that the Waltons, the Godseys, and the Baldwin sisters all accept Stanley at face value for who he is. They don't judge him when they learn of his past illness. Slowly, through their help and acceptance, we see this broken and lost man restored to a new life.

JULIET LAW PACKER, WRITER

Poor Mr. Perkins suffered a nervous breakdown and was away from the mountain for a while. When he came back he stopped to see me and he was shaking just dreadfully. I went to the cupboard

(I had made him some tea) and got a bottle and put a splash of "recipe" in it. He stopped shaking!

PEGGY REA, ACTOR (ROSE BURTON)

The Beginning

Air date: 3/05/81; Writer: Kathleen Hite; Director: Lawrence Dobkin
Tom Marshall, the new minister, arrives on the mountain and gets the attention of his complacent congregation by ringing the church bell in the middle of the night. Toni moves into the Baldwin sisters' home and, over dinner, Jason mentions that she is Jewish. After a discussion with the new minister, she and Jason eventually decide to get married.

> *The love of my life, Lisa Harrison, joined the cast as Jason's feisty girlfriend, Toni Hazelton. The character was inspired by a song I had written, "Antoinette," which Lisa and I used to perform with our band. Even though our song gave the character her name, Lisa was among a large group of actresses called in for two days of auditions for the role. Needless to say, we were both thrilled when she was cast in the part. When we shot Lisa's first episode I was so concerned about her having a good experience—having fun, coming off well in our scenes, etc., that I completely forgot to concentrate on my own performance. I kept flubbing lines and bumping into the furniture. Of course, Lisa was great. Luckily, I had her there to pull me through!*

JON WALMSLEY, ACTOR (JASON WALTON)

The Pearls

Air date: 3/12/81; Writer: Mary Worrell; Director: James Sheldon
Corabeth is in Doe Hill when her twin sister, Orma Lee, drops in on Ike. The sisters had not been friendly in the past but healed their wounds and became best of friends. Elizabeth feels lonely for her parents and runs off to the bus station to begin her adventure to Arizona, but Jason tells her that this is not a good time to visit. He promises to take her himself at a later time.

> *It is difficult to name which episode I enjoyed the most. It was so much fun to play Corabeth, as well as her sister, in "The Pearls," but also to play such varied roles as a recovering alcoholic and in*

another show to become a parent when we adopted Aimee, but perhaps most memorable is the first show when I was introduced into the Walton clan.

RONNIE CLAIRE EDWARDS, ACTOR (CORABETH GODSEY)

Ronnie Claire Edwards is a riot in this episode where she plays herself as well as her sister, Orma Lee. The true spirit of this fine actress comes through in her wacky portrayal of both roles.

DUANE SHELL, FAN—LOS ANGELES, CALIFORNIA

The Victims

Air date: 3/19/81; Writer: Juliet Packer; Director: Lawrence Dobkin
Kenny and Laurie have a troubled marriage full of physical violence. The Waltons intercede on behalf of Laurie and she stays with them. Kenny arrives with a shotgun and threatens to get even. Jim-Bob invests in war surplus but can't seem to make a profit. He is forced to sell his car to pay the loan. He receives an offer from a film company that wants to buy the surplus as props for a film.

This was a dark episode about men returning from war who are casualties themselves, unable to deal with the memories that haunt them. At the center of the story arced two guest characters: Laurie and Kenny Ellis, a young husband back from active duty and his loyal wife. John-Boy, Erin, Jason, and Mary Ellen all try to protect Laurie from Kenny as he becomes increasingly abusive. At the climax Kenny slips out of reality and believes he is surrounded by Nazis. John-Boy brings him back to reality, but we know that Kenny remains deeply psychically wounded. Although this was not my favorite episode, I think it will remain timely as long as there are wars and violence.

JULIET LAW PACKER, WRITER

The Threshold

Air date: 4/02/81; Writer: Scott Hamner; Director: Herbert Hirschmann
Dean Beck, at Boatwright University, asks John-Boy to do an introductory television show for the Board of Trustees to teach them the value of the new medium. Zuleika Dunbar sets her sights on

Stanley, much to the concern of Rose. Jim-Bob builds a TV set and the family is able to see John-Boy's television premiere.

> *I had a lot of fun writing "The Thresold." The historical research that went into telling the story of Boatwright University's fledgling television show was extremely interesting, as was the production company's re-creation of an early television studio and broadcast. I played with the characters' attitudes about this technological marvel, and John-Boy's enthusiasm was met with stalwart resistance by those who insisted television was a passing fad and would never measure up to radio. The "B" story was about Rose going on a diet in order to keep the affection of her beau, Stanley, when Zuleika Dunbar decides to win him away from her. In the end, Stanley remains true to Rose, and Rose learns not to compare her "insides" to other people's "outsides."*
>
> SCOTT HAMNER, WRITER

> *I will never forget this episode. It was directed by a marvelous sweet man named Herb Hirschmann. You may know that in shooting film it is customary when shooting a close-up for both actors in the scene to stay close and repeat their lines even though the camera may only be on one actor. There was a darling scene in this episode where my grandson Jeffrey climbs into bed with me to tell me he doesn't believe in Santa Claus anymore. When it was time for my close-up to be shot, Jeffrey's alloted time (set by rules governing child actors) had run out. So Herb Hirschmann climbed in bed with me and said, "Sorry, Peg, you'll have to do the scene with me!" I reveal this story to clear up any misunderstandings in Hollywood about my once having been in bed with my director!*
>
> PEGGY REA, ACTOR (ROSE BURTON)

The Indiscretion

Air date: 5/07/81; Writer: E. F. Wallengren; Director: James Sheldon
Ike and Corabeth argue over an old letter to Ike from another woman. Corabeth files for divorce, but Ike finally convinces her that nothing really happened and he has always been faithful to her. Elizabeth and Drew plan to spend a romantic night together, but she backs out at the last minute.

The marriage of
Stanley Perkins
(William Shallert) and
Rose Burton (Peggy
Rea).

The Heartache

Air date: 5/14/81; Writer: Kathleen Hite; Director: Herbert Hirschmann
Stanley Perkins again asks Rose to be his bride and she accepts.
Rose has been experiencing chest pains and is finally convinced
by Mary Ellen to see a doctor. The doctor informs her that she
has a heart condition and she suddenly cancels the wedding.
Stanley and the family eventually determine what has happened
and the wedding proceeds as scheduled. Cindy decides she
would rather be a housewife and quits her job.

The Lumberjack

Air date: 5/21/81; Writer: Carol Zeitz; Director: Harvey S. Laidman
Ike buys a Geiger counter and he and Jim-Bob search the mountain for uranium. Paul Northridge, the son of a prominent lumberman, meets Erin and they have a whirlwind romance. Paul and his father constantly argue but with the help of Erin are able to settle their differences.

The Hostage

Air date: 5/28/81; Writer: Marjorie Fowler; Director: Herbert Hirschmann
A fourteen-year-old mountain girl is promised in marriage but Mary Ellen interferes, saying the girl is too young. Mary Ellen hides the girl in a nearby area. In retaliation, the groom-to-be kidnaps Elizabeth to force the return of his bride-to-be. Meanwhile, the Baldwins' cousin, Octavia, comes for a visit and causes trouble wherever she goes.

The Revel

Air date: 6/04/81; Writer: Scott Hamner; Director: Harry Harris
John-Boy, living in New York, runs short of money and appeals to his publisher for help. They give him some money so that he can write his second book. The Baldwin sisters plan a party for their old friends and classmates but the invitations are returned. Everyone is either too old, dead, or lives far away. The Waltons come to the rescue when they and their friends show up and the party is held. This was the last scheduled episode of the series.

> *Our family came from a culture rich in the tradition of story-telling. The Waltons was based on characters introduced in the Christmas special* The Homecoming, *which in turn incorporated a tall tale my grandfather told my father and his siblings when they were children and which my father told my sister and me when we were very small. It was one of my favorite stories as a child and I was delighted when it became a novella and then the television special, which led to the creation of the weekly series. I grew up watching and eventually participating in the dramatization of our family mythology. I was very honored to write the last*

James Hamner

episode of the series, and to me it was a kind of symbolic act of "taking up the torch" from my father and embracing storytelling as a profession. "The Revel" exemplified core values espoused in the show: the celebration of family and the rising above individual differences for the greater good.

SCOTT HAMNER, WRITER

... JIM-BOB HAS THE LAST WORD!

When Earl asked me to come up with a favorite episode I spent a month looking back and could not settle on one. To pick a favorite would almost be like asking if I have a favorite brother or sister or family member, and that sure isn't going to happen! What I would say is that all of the shows were my favorites in the way they depicted a certain family member, character, or event that touched our lives in some way. The love of our family was present in every show. The deaths, marriages, and births, the deer and turkey hunts and the fishing trips were all a part of our lives. The reporting of the death of Roosevelt was especially poignant. I still remember going to Rockfish as the train bearing his body with Eleanor in the last car passed through. The beginning of World War II, the burning of the Hindenburg, the removal of families from up in the mountain as documented in "The Conflict," were also a part of our lives. These are history lessons and should be cherished by everyone. There was also lots of humor. The funny moment that stands out most for me is Grandma helping John-Boy with his sermon when he fills in for Reverend Fordwick. I often wondered if Ellen Corby might have caused herself to get blood clots from pounding her fist on the dresser, which could have led to her stroke. Heart-wrenching moments were many, and the one I remember most was when John-Boy pulled the Bible from the fire and Mrs. Brimmer trans-

Goodnight John-Boy

lated and read from it. How could I pick one favorite when each episode was "one of my favorites"?

JAMES HAMNER, MODEL FOR JIM-BOB

Specials (1982–1997)

A Wedding on Walton's Mountain

Air date: 1982; Writers: Marjorie Fowler and Claylene Jones; Director: Lee Philips

Erin falls in love with Paul Northridge and he promises to build her a dream house on the mountain. Jonesy and Mary Ellen prepare for the grand opening of his new veterinary clinic. Ashley Longworth Jr. unexpectedly returns to the mountain. His wife has died and he has come to ask Erin's hand. John returns from Arizona to oversee Ben's dealings at the mill. Reverend Tom Marshall returns to the mountain with his new bride. Paul and Erin marry at the church with Grandma looking on.

Mary McDonough.

"Jonesy," as played by
Richard Gilliand.

In this two-hour special in which my character gets married, I wore the same beautiful dress in which my own mother had been married. My mother decided to make a gift of it to the museum at Schuyler, and we went there together to present it to the museum. It is a part of their permanent display.

MARY MCDONOUGH, ACTOR (ERIN WALTON)

Mother's Day on Walton's Mountain

Air date: 1982; Writers: Marjorie Fowler and Claylene Jones; Director: Gwen Arner

Mary Ellen weds Arlington Westcott Jones III, and they leave for a honeymoon of camping under the stars. Corabeth and daughter Aimee develop a difficult relationship over her choice of clothes and her dating in college. While Jonesy fishes, Mary Ellen flips over the car and is rushed to the hospital for surgery. Dr. Cole tells Mary Ellen that he repaired her uterus and it would be risky for her to have any more children. Elizabeth and Drew are having problems and Aimee flirts with him. Cindy delivers a son, Charles Benjamin Walton. Mary Ellen travels to Arizona to visit with her mother.

I felt very honored to write this special two-hour episode. The show centers around the newly married Mary Ellen's reaction to the news that she can't have any more children. Her new husband, Jonesy, was played by Richard Gilliand, who brought tremendous warmth to the role. When watching the show for the first time, even though I knew exactly what was going to happen, I still wanted to scream at Mary Ellen, "Tell your husband! He can handle it! Don't shut him out!" But she is afraid. Rather than share the news she withdraws. The healing begins only after Mary Ellen is able to visit and express her fears to her mother.

There were several subplots, most notably having to do with Ben and Cindy having their second baby. This put me in a unique position. I had written the show when Cindy had her first child, and since I was writing the episode I was able to name her Virginia (Ginny) after my own mother. Now Cindy had a boy, and

I was able to name him Charles after my father. I had always felt like a Walton, but I believe this episode made it official.

JULIET LAW PACKER, WRITER

A Day of Thanks on Walton's Mountain

Air date: 1982; Writer: Kathleen Hite; Director: Harry Harris

Just a few days before Thanksgiving, John Curtis has met a mysterious friend in the woods who ultimately turns out to be the spirit of Grandpa still looking after the family. Jim-Bob and Yancy buy some government surplus that turns out to be a bad deal. Ben talks to his father in Arizona and wishes he could be home for Thanksgiving, and he does come home. Suffering from writer's block, John-Boy returns to the mountain to rejuvenate his spirit. Paul and Erin are having marital problems, and he asks her to move into an old cabin in the woods with him to find each other again. The Thanksgiving festivities continue with Ike, Corabeth, the Baldwin sisters, and Yancy coming to dinner with the family.

It appears that everybody is going to be away from the ancestral home for Thanksgiving, but one by one they find their way home to be with the family. It's one of the special two-hour movies, which was shown long after the regular run was over. Coming together to work again, it brought home to me what a close-knit family we actors had become and how much we had become like members of a real family. The relationships were so real that we called Ellen Grandma and she gave us each presents on our birthdays. And I remember that when the series was coming to an end Ralph and Michael, who had been our parents on film, tried to help us realize that the end of the series did not necessarily mean that our relationships had to end too. We are still close, and since the show closed we have gone through marriages, divorces, and death, and if anything we have become even closer over the years.

MARY McDONOUGH, ACTOR (ERIN WALTON)

A Walton Thanksgiving Reunion

Air date: 1993; Writers: Rod Peterson and Claire Whitaker; Director: Harry Harris

It is 1963 and John-Boy is a TV reporter in New York City. They are planning a trip to Walton's Mountain to introduce Janet to the family. Jim-Bob is a pilot doing crop-dusting and charter flights. Ben and John are partners in the mill but have a very different approach to business. John still wants to build the "dream house" on the mountain and realizes that this will be their last Thanksgiving in the old house. Drew and Elizabeth rekindle their romance and he goes to work at the mill. The Baldwin sisters are arrested for selling bootleg whiskey. President Kennedy is killed and John-Boy leaves for Washington, D.C., to report on the events. After Thanksgiving dinner, the family gathers in front of the TV to watch John-Boy's report on the assassination. About that time he comes in saying that his report was videotaped. Later that night John-Boy announces that he and Janet are getting married.

> *One of the strongest memories I have is of the empathy I felt for Cindy in this reunion special. She was experiencing heartbreaking infertility. I too was experiencing infertility and was equally heart-broken. I was able to let go of some of my personal pain through my portrayal of hers. It was an amazing experience, and it must have helped because six months later I was joyously pregnant with my first child!*

LESLIE WINSTON, ACTOR (CINDY WALTON)

A Walton Wedding

Air date: 1995; Writers: Rod Peterson and Claire Whitaker; Director: Robert Ellis Miller
In New York, Janet's aunt Flo assumes responsibility for Janet and John-Boy's wedding plans and turns the event into a major production. John-Boy has written an article about Grandma's stroke and his editor encourages him to return to the mountain for more research. He returns home and moves into the quiet cabin near Drucilla's Pond. Janet makes a surprise appearance and announces that she has fired Aunt Flo. John and the townspeople are concerned about a subdivision planned for the area. John-Boy and Janet are married while Toni has a baby in the next room. John-Boy and Janet paddle across Drucilla's Pond to begin their honeymoon.

A Walton Easter

Air date: 1997; Writer: Julie Sayres; Director: Robert Ellis Miller
John-Boy reports live on the moon landing. Random House
Publishing decides to send a reporter, Aurora Jeffries, with Janet
and John-Boy when they visit Walton's Mountain. Janet is expecting her first child in about a month. Elizabeth makes a surprise
visit and announces that she is home for good. Drew announces to
Elizabeth that he had a girlfriend. John-Boy tells Janet that he
might want to relocate to the mountain. Mary Ellen is checking
Janet's vital signs and announces that she can hear two heartbeats.
Drew and Elizabeth become engaged. Janet gives birth to a boy
and a girl.

*The first thing I remember about writing two of the Walton
reunion movies was my initial meeting with Earl Hamner. Rich
Heller, one of the producers, brought me in to the project and
arranged a lunch for me to meet Earl and talk about the direction
of the movie. When I arrived at the restaurant, Rich and Earl
were already there, and gentlemen that they were, they rose to
greet me. When Earl said hello and started to talk I had an immediate visceral reaction. That was the voice I knew so well from all
my years of watching* The Waltons *as a kid. He was John-Boy, all
grown up. He was warm and engaging, responsive to my ideas,
and I walked away from that lunch eager to get started on the
script.*

*Before we started shooting, we had a table reading, where
all the actors sit around and read the script. For me, sitting
around that table with all those shockingly familiar faces was
thrilling. There sat Ralph Waite, Michael Learned, Richard
Thomas, and all the kids, now grown up and many with children of their own. Their faces and voices were so deeply etched
into my past, and here they were sitting at a table saying my
words. As the shooting progressed I was impressed by the profes-
sionalism of all those actors. They knew their lines, they knew
their characters, and there were no prima donnas. The director
was also a delight, welcoming me to the set every day and*

John-Boy and Janet's wedding.

including me in the process. This does not always happen to writers.

Once shooting starts, the writer is usually persona non grata on the set. A Walton Easter was the total opposite. The atmosphere on the set was fun, warm, and relaxed. And the movie, I feel, reflected the collaborative process that seemed to work as it should, and often doesn't. We were all proud of the finished project, and it remains a joyous memory of the most fun I've ever had working as a screenwriter.

JULIE SAYRES, WRITER

Chapter Six

Walton's Mountain Museum

❧

"Our Gathering Place"

W ALTON FANS ACROSS AMERICA AND around the world will be forever grateful to Dr. Heywood Greenberg, better known as "Woody," and to the people of Schuyler, Virginia.

Woody, a former county commissioner, had a dream that would benefit Nelson County and especially the village of Schuyler, the home of Earl Hamner Jr., creator of our beloved Walton family.

Woody blew the breath of life into the idea of having a Walton's Mountain museum. His idea ignited a spark, and the people of Schuyler contributed time, money, labor, antiques, and devotion to an idea that resulted in one of the finest nonprofit tourist attractions in America, according to avid Walton fans.

With a $30,000 rural grant from the state and another special gift, plus a tremendous volunteer effort from the folk of Schuyler, Virginia, the 1925 brick former elementary school was converted into the Walton's Mountain Museum.

Since the opening of the museum in October 1992, more than 250,000 Walton fans from all over the world have journeyed to the quaint little village of 400 residents.

Your heart is filled with nostalgia as you take a leisurely stroll through the museum. Their reproduction of the Waltons' 1930s-era home is unbelievable! There's John-Boy's famous bedroom with his desk, spectacles, and his "Big Chief" writing tablet in which he so lovingly recorded his heartfelt secrets.

As you enter the living room, where old-fashioned lace curtains grace the windows, you can almost sense the presence of our beloved Waltons as they would gather for a time of "togetherness" to play games or listen to the radio.

The 1930s-era kitchen is a sight to be treasured forever. The biscuits on the stove look so real that you are tempted to eat one. As you stand in awe listening to the tour guide, you can almost smell Olivia's applesauce cake permeating the atmosphere. Ike Godsey's store is another highlight of the tour.

A visit to the Walton's Mountain Museum will take you into yesterday and into the embodiment of Woody Greenberg's dream.

CAROLYN GRINNELL, PRESIDENT OF THE WALTONS
INTERNATIONAL FAN CLUB

The Grand Opening

The Walton's Mountain Museum opened on October 24, 1992. Almost six thousand fans and guests were on hand for the daylong celebration. The museum is housed in the Schuyler Community Center, a former elementary school.

Schuyler is nestled in the Blue Ridge Mountains of central Virginia. A white frame house in the center of town was the boyhood home of Earl Hamner, the creator of *The Waltons*.

Earl Hamner, his brothers and sisters, several of the show's writers and producers, and numerous cast members reunited for the occasion. The festivities included a presentation in the school auditorium in the morning and an open-air program after lunch. The

Ralph Waite (John Walton) at the museum's grand opening.

Goodnight John-Boy

Robert Brent Hall, the museum's curator, with Earl Hamner.

cast members mingled with the fans, signed autographs, and seemed genuinely taken with the crowd's affection.

Visitors can tour the rooms, watch a *Waltons* videotape prepared especially for the museum, and shop in the re-creation of Ike Godsey's store. The store features hundreds of items, many made by local craftspeople from the Schuyler area.

The museum is open daily from the first Saturday in March through the last Sunday in November (exceptions: Easter, Thanksgiving, and the second Saturday in October). Visiting hours are from 10 A.M. to 4 P.M. Handicapped services and assistance are available.

Museum Dedication

On March 1, 1997, hundreds of visitors and guests joined Earl Hamner and his family in dedicating a plaque to Earl's parents. The following remarks were made by Earl on that occasion:

> Good morning. Welcome to the Walton Museum. Welcome to Schuyler and welcome to Nelson County. This is a very special day for me and my brothers and sisters, and we thank you for coming to share it with us.
>
> Just being in this building opens a flood of memories. I went to the fourth grade in that room. Mrs. Strickland was my teacher. Mrs. Ben Giannini taught the

Dedicated to the memory of
our Mother and Father
whose love for each other
and for their family
is celebrated in this Museum.

Earl Hamner, Jr.　　　　　Paul Louis Hamner
Clifton Anderson Hamner　Willard Harold Hamner
Marion Hamner Hawkes　　James Edmund Hamner
Audrey J. Hamner　　　　　Nancy Hamner Jamerson

sixth grade right over there, and I graduated from Miss Clyde Parr's room there in the back. And I stood right here in 1940 when I graduated and gave a speech. It had a lot do with the promise of America and little premonition that the following year the world we knew would be changed forever by war.

Another memory of those years comes back from time to time. There was a graduation dance held here in the auditorium. I was desperately in love at the time with Miss Elsie Mayo, who taught the seventh grade. Mostly my love took the form of adoring her from a distance, but I finally got to dance with her. The music was a song called "Careless" and the words went: "Careless, now that you've got me loving you." I remember singing the words as we danced but Miss Mayo didn't seem to notice. I suppose she had no idea of the degree of my passion, nor did she ever know how broken my heart was when she married the math teacher, Mr. T. Dan Gusmerotti.

We are here today to honor my mother and father, but in so doing I would like us to honor all the mothers and fathers of their generation, especially those families of Schuyler who have come such a long distance in Schuyler's history.

I have always wondered who the first settlers might have been to come to this part of Virginia. I imagine the very first were hunters and trappers who came even before the Revolutionary or the French and Indian Wars. People from the Tidewater who felt the need to push their way farther into the continent. People who wanted to be near mountains. Later came the farmers, the preachers, the schoolteachers, men with families, and explorers. Certainly they were an adventuresome lot; they had to be resourceful; they had to be people with a strong sense of independence and self-reliance; they had to be brave people who weren't afraid of hard work or danger or the unknown. They had to be men and women of strong will and strong minds. We are their descendants, and we come from strong stuff.

In their names you can still hear the sounds of many countries, the accents of those hardy souls who sailed in small ships from the shores of Ireland. There are English names of those who left families and loved ones behind on the teeming streets of London and Liverpool. Even today the names are reminiscent of German names that remind us of those German Baptists who came here looking for religious liberty, along with Quakers and Mennonites, and even Italian names like my Giannini forebears. I wish I could say my ancestors came looking for religious liberty. Actually they came over here to grow grapes and make wine, and there's been a noticeable thirst running in the family ever since.

Even today those of us who were born and raised in this area still carry the sounds of the Scottish people who settled here and left a strong imprint on our speech. We still say "out" and "house" and "mouse" and "about." It always surprised me when I left Schuyler to learn that I "talked funny."

At one time early settlers came to Schuyler looking for gold, and for a while a gold mine was actually worked here. But the real gold they found here was the generous earth, the beauty of our streams and rivers and the richness of our forests. The Cosby family came early, and so did the Eubanks and the Dwyers. They found friendly people, people who made good neighbors, people like themselves, people who had values. They had names like Shoemaker, and Walker, and Goolsby, and Beasley, and Kidd. The Hardings came early and so did the Tylers, and Thackers, and the Maupins, and the Ownsbys.

Soapstone was the key that opened the door to a flood of people. A large deposit of soapstone had been discovered as early as 1800, and soapstone brought the Belmore family, and the Rothwells, and the Carrols, and the Fortunes. The soapstone became commercially important when quarrying began, and later when the Alberene Stone Company merged with the Virginia Stone Company, we were on our way to the big time. Back in those early days, surprisingly, Schuyler had something in common with New York City. We both had a Riverside Drive. Thank God, the resemblance to New York City stopped right there.

I've always loved the names of the people who came to live in Schuyler. They had names like Tillman, and Drumheller, and Moore, and Via, and Bryant. They had names like Branch, and Dameron, and Purvis. Many of their descendants still call Schuyler home, such as Gentry, and Banton, and Morris, and Norvell, and Burton, and Winebarger. The sound of their names is a roll call of those people who made Schuyler the good place it has always been—the Sprouses, the Gardeners, the Witts, and the Pontons. People who are the backbone of the country, the people I grew up with and went to school with. Phillipses, and Crists, and Raglands, and Halls, and Wades, and Mayos, and Goolsbys, Crickenbergers, Sprouses, and Wrays, and Allens, and Saunders. Good names. Good neighbors. Let us remember and honor all these families.

In every country around the world that has a television station, this community, this small village in the heart of Nelson County, has come to be synonymous with family values. I think I had something to do with spreading that news, and I'm proud of that. But I can't take credit for those values themselves. They came from our parents, the people who nurtured us and who passed on to us the notions that there was dignity in work, satisfaction in having a job and doing it well, that we can and must be self-reliant and resourceful, that our country's laws are to be obeyed, that we have a right to practice the religion of our choice, the belief that our parents and grandparents not only deserve respect, but are to be treasured for the rituals and stories and rules of conduct that we all need to know and to pass on to our children if we are to call ourselves civilized.

We didn't corner the market on these values, and I think they are more prevalent throughout our country than books and television and the movies would have us believe. We would be foolish to deny that drugs and crime and scandal have taken their toll on us. But I believe that there is still more Judeo-Christianity than crime in this country, that there is more hope than heroin, more virtue than violence, and more good than evil.

If those values have been weakened today, they sustained our parents and their generation through some often mean and troublesome times. Looking back on our parents' generation, it is striking how often their lives were shadowed by war.

Their own parents more often than not grew up in the shadow of those years following the Civil War. To my knowledge nobody around here owned plantations or slaves, but still the economic hardships and social upheaval that followed that war weighed heavily on our grandparents' lives and were part of our own parents' heritage.

Our mothers and fathers were children or in their early teens when World War I came about. A few of them were old enough to go to Europe and some of them didn't make it back. But the young men of Schuyler and now the young women have always been there when our country needed them.

Again, in World War II, our parents were called on to send their sons and daughters to fight in Europe and in the Pacific. The first life to be lost from Schuyler in World War II was Goldman Moore, the son of Charles and Mabel Moore. Later, Raymond Branch was killed in the line of duty. Raymond was the son of Billy and Maude Branch. Our country called again during the Vietnam War, and once again the people of Nelson County answered that call. Ronnie Crizer, the son of Arlene and Charley Crizer, gave his life in that war as did Tinsley Bryant, the son of Tom and Eva Bryant. These wars gave a special and tragic meaning to our parents' generation. Having fought for their country, having given their sons and daughters to their country, I think they came to appreciate the deeper meaning of love of country, of honor and of sacrifice.

Another formidable event shadowed the people of our parents' generation: the Great Depression of the late 1920s and early '30s. The Depression made them frugal, and more often than not they passed that quality down to their children. The Depression called on our parents to be resourceful, and they passed some of that quality on down to us. Clothing was handed down from the oldest to the youngest. Sometimes a boy's shirt landed on one of the girls, and the pants didn't quite fit that younger brother, but if we complained my mother always said, "They're clean, and you'll wear them!"

Our parents were resourceful in feeding us too. We all kept pigs and had a cow out grazing somewhere. I am probably the only writer in Hollywood who knows how to milk a cow. Every family back in those Depression years had a garden, and during the summer our mothers and grandmothers put up vegetables and berries and fruit. I can still remember that wonderful vinegary aroma that permeated the house after the first frost when my mother picked the last of the tomatoes and made green tomato relish. My grandmother Giannini's peach preserves were probably the best in the country, and the sausage they made when we slaughtered hogs was so pungent and peppery, it makes me hungry just to think of it.

And while our mothers and grandmothers did the canning, our fathers shot quail and pheasant, venison and squirrel, and rabbit. They brought back bass and catfish from the Rockfish River and at Thanksgiving there was never a store-bought turkey, but one that came from the neighboring hills and woods. We knew it came from that flock over on Wales's Mountain because it still had birdshot in it.

This building was a beacon of light in this community. While many of our parents had had little opportunity for schooling, most of them respected learning and yearned for at least a high school education for their children.

And I will never forget my father's pride when I won a scholarship to the University of Richmond. He even gave me his one white shirt, although he did say to my mother: "What am I going to be buried in if I die while he's down yonder in Richmond strutting around in my good shirt?"

I want to tell you one of our favorite family stories about my mother and father. My mother's mother, Miss Ora Lee Giannini, was Baptist. And she was about as Baptist as you can get. She disapproved of dancing, swearing, card playing, handholding, overly long kisses or any public display of affection, and raised voices on the Sabbath.

The last person in the world she would have selected as a suitor for her sixteen-year-old daughter was our father. He was twenty at the time, a known carouser, a gambler, a drinker, a dancer, a crack shot and, befitting his Welsh ancestry, he was a singer of note. He thought nothing of going hunting on Sunday and even worse, when he defiled the Lord's Day by fishing he had to go right past the Baptist Church to get to the Rockfish River. In the church they'd be singing "Shall We Gather at the River?" and going past he'd smile and nod in complete agreement.

My grandmother forbade my mother to see my father, but somehow they managed to have a courtship. My father proposed. My mother accepted, and they sneaked off to Lovingston to get the license. That night, when she was supposed to be at choir practice, my mother met my father and they went to the Baptist Parsonage to ask Preacher Hicks to marry them. Preacher Hicks had a mild stutter, which became intense if he was under stress. He was now under stress. He knew that my grandmother would have a fit if he married the two young people. When my father presented him with the license, Preacher Hicks said, "I cannot marry you." To which my father replied: "You're not the only damn preacher in the country. We'll find us another one."

At that point Preacher Hicks said, "Under the c-circumstances, I will marry you," and so he did.

Neighbors predicted that the marriage wouldn't last six months. Her mother swore never to speak to her daughter again, but you know mothers. She came around and saw that gradually her daughter had tamed her young man. He mended his ways, he got himself baptized and joined the church, and he said good-bye to his fast friends. They had forty-five good years together and to his dying day, he called our mother "Sweetheart."

Our youngest sister, Nancy Hamner Jamerson, will unveil the plaque in their honor, and I'll ask Jim Hamner to read the dedication: "Dedicated to the memory of our

Mother and Father whose love for each other and for their family is celebrated in this Museum."

So this day we honor our mother and father and all the other mothers and fathers from Schuyler of their generations. How fortunate we were to have had them. How rich we are because of them.

EARL HAMNER

Goodnight John-Boy

Chapter Seven

Tribute

❧

ALEX VAN HAREN (THE NETHERLANDS). Karen Kearney (Australia). Irene Porter (England). Dorothy Phillips (Canada). Carolyn Grinnell (USA). What do all these people have in common? They are fans of *The Waltons*!

From the beginning, when the cynics predicted the series would fail, the fans proved them wrong. People found the series. They were touched, or moved, or just entertained. They told their friends and those friends told other friends until the family from the backwoods of Virginia was number one in the ratings and had supporters all over the world.

Over the years, we who have been part of the show have received thousands and thousands of appreciative letters from the audience. It has been impossible to thank each person individually. Most of the letters expressed a feeling of gratitude and a longing to experience in their own lives the same thing the Walton family experienced each week.

The feelings fans have had for the show were summed up recently in an article written for the the *Raleigh News and Observer* by Elaine Klonicki. We reprint Elaine's essay here as a tribute to those people who kept the series on the air from the beginning and who continue to find solace and inspiration and enjoyment in *The Waltons.*

What's Your Reality?

As the television networks announce another round of "reality programming," I find myself pining for *The Waltons,* a family show from the 1970s. Over the years, people have come to either love or hate *The Waltons,* which ran for nine years and received numerous Emmys. I am in the former category. I loved it from the time I first saw the pilot episode, called *The Homecoming,* when it aired as a Christmas special in December of 1971. I too was a member of a large family reared by parents with strong values and religious faith. I was the youngest of eight children and like little Elizabeth on the show, sometimes felt overwhelmed and lost in the crowd. As with the Waltons, money was tight for us and we learned to make good use of the resources we had. When you're young though, you never quite appreciate the blessings you have, and so I often longed to belong to the Walton family instead of my own. The grandparents were fun-loving, the parents affectionate, the older brothers sweet and sensitive, and everyone really talked about their feelings.

In *The Waltons,* the character of writer Earl Hamner Jr. was called John-Boy, and he was the oldest son. No matter what John-Boy experienced in a particular story, each episode was wrapped up nicely in Hamner's own voice, expressing gratitude for his family and the values he was taught growing up in the Blue Ridge Mountains of Virginia during the Depression. Those tributes were often the most touching parts of the show. Critics called *The Waltons* saccharine and unrealistic, but the family members weren't portrayed as perfect, and they faced many challenges. They often stumbled along the way, even the adults, but each family member struggled hard to live life under the framework of the family's principles and values. Honesty, hard work, respect, responsibility, self-sacrifice, compassion, and kindness—today they package it and call it "character education."

In dramatic contrast, the "reality shows" of today entertain by highlighting the worst human character traits: temptation, lust, greed, and distrust. Some claim that art is just imitating life here, but surely we know that the imitation goes both ways. Some aspects of life are definitely not worth capturing on film, and particularly not to be offered as a steady diet to young, impressionable minds.

Growing up, I used to wish that I had been born in an earlier time. I imagined that the world was simpler and the people better behaved. I believed my parents and their friends when they bemoaned the state of the world. But I've lived awhile since then, and studied some history and psychology and philosophy. I know now that good and evil exist in every era, and how you see the world depends a lot on how you look at it. My kids know that I choose to see the glass as half full rather than half empty.

Quite a while back, it seems now, I made a conscious decision that my world would be a good, kind, generous world because that's what I'd be looking for. Everywhere I seek evidence of kind words, kind deeds, honesty, and happy coincidences. And I find it, even on television, on Arts and Entertainment, Animal Planet, Home and Garden TV, The History Channel, The Learning Channel, The Travel Channel, and public television.

For as much as I sometimes wished to be in a different family, I realize now that my parents did just fine when it came to teaching us values in a loving way. They did it in the same way that the Waltons did, one teachable moment at a time, in everyday-life experiences when they admonished us to "do the right thing." We shared many happy times and rough times, and still do. Like John-Boy, I'm finding myself increasingly grateful for my upbringing, and for many other things in my life, and increasingly respectful of the natural beauty of this Earth, which is highlighted on the show.

So don't ask me if I've seen *Temptation Island* or *Survivor II* or *The Mole*. I'll be watching re-runs of *The Waltons*. The fact that thousands of people visit the Walton's Museum in Schuyler, Virginia, each year means that I'm not the only one. If you find yourself feeling dissatisfied and disillusioned with the world after watching reality programming, consider that the reality you're seeing is not the reality you may be looking for.

Printed with permission of the author, Elaine Klonicki. Elaine is a free-lance writer with a B.A. in psychology from North Carolina State University. Her mission is to inspire others to live a more joyful, purposeful life. Her new book, Thinking About Therapy? What to Expect from "The Talking Cure," *is available on-line or ask your local bookseller. Permission is also granted by Allen Torrey, op-ed editor, the* News and Observer.

Chapter Eight

Resources

❧

Fan Clubs

Friends of the Waltons

The Friends of the Waltons is a division of the Walton's Mountain Museum. Members receive a quarterly newsletter, free admission to the Museum and a 10 percent discount on all purchases in the museum store or by mail-order.

- Annual Individual Memberships are $15 per person (U.S.); $17 per person (outside the U.S.).
- Annual Family Memberships are $25 (U.S.) and $27 (outside the U.S.). The family membership covers both spouses and children eighteen and under.

Friends of The Waltons
The Walton's Mountain Museum
P.O. Box 124
Schuyler, VA 22969
434-831-2000
Email: waltonmt@cstone.net

The Waltons International Fan Club

Started in 1992, at the dedication of the Walton's Mountain Museum, the Fan Club publishes a quarterly newsletter and holds an annual reunion. Dues are $20 per year (U.S.). The Fan Club also publishes a cookbook. For further information, contact:

Carolyn Grinnell, President
The Waltons International Fan Club
P.O. Box 1055
Kernersville, NC 27285
336-993-2752
Email: olivia@viafamily.com

The Waltons Friendship Society

The logo of the Waltons Friendship Society (*above*) depicts the open window of John-Boy's bedroom showing a book and lighted lamp.

The Waltons Friendship Society (WFS) was begun in England in 1990 and reorganized in 1992 by Ray Knight and Irene Porter. Ray, Irene, and the almost one hundred other members of the Society are avid Waltons fans. The Society publishes a quarterly newsletter called *MAILBOX*. Subscriptions are $20 per year (U.S.).

Send all correspondence to:

Irene Porter, Waltons Friendship Society
Riding Gate House, Riding Gate
Wincanton, Somerset
BA9 8NG
England
Email: Ijohnrene@cs.com

Internet Resources

www.the-waltons.com
   The Waltons Web site

www.pollysbedandbreakfast.com/index.html
   Polly's Bed and Breakfast in Schuyler, Virginia

www.angelfire.com/tv/homecoming
   Web site for *The Homecoming*

www.indianahistory.org/pub/traces/geer.html
   Indiana Historical Society Web site (learn more about Will Geer)

www.theatricum.com
   The Will Geer Theatricum Botanicum Web site

www.geocities.com/heartland/meadows/7604/webring.html
   Add your site to the *Waltons* Web ring or visit Web ring sites.

www.nelsoncounty.com
   The Nelson County Office of Tourism

www.galesburg.net/~atkins/waltons.html
   An excellent *Waltons* Web site from Bill Atkins

email: dotp@mail.on.rogers.wave.ca
   Send email to Dorothy Phillips in Canada and join her chat room

www.collectors-cabinet.com/tvhouse.htm
   Want to buy a replica of the Waltons' house?

www.miniscape.com/waltonphotos1.htm
   The Waltons by Fumiyo and Dave Selner

www.jimtvc.com
   Jim's Collectibles has TV memorabilia for sale, including items from *The Waltons*.

www.geocities.com/TelevisionCity/3436/
   83 Blue Ridge Parkway: The Waltons Interactive (designed and hosted by Alex and Marca Van Haren)

www.geocities.com/TelevisionCity/2792/walton1.htm
   Visit Karen Kearney's *Waltons* site in Australia and join Karen's Digest Mailing List.

geocities.com/TelevisionCity/Set/4536/pastdigests.html
> Karen Kearney has posted her past Digests on this delightful site.

www.eonline.com
> E! Online; contains filmographies of the cast.

www.ebay.com
> An auction site that frequently features *Waltons* memorabilia for sale

www.the-waltons.com/pbs.html
> Web site for the *Waltons* special on PBS

www.waltonmuseum.org
> Web site for the Walton's Mountain Museum

email: waltonmt@cstone.net
> Send email to the museum.

http://webpages.marshall.edu/~irby2/waltons
> Brenda Irby's tribute to *The Waltons*

www.bbctv-ap.freeserve.co.uk/wltnp1.htm
> Arthur Dungate's miscellany page

www.geocities.com/TelevisionCity/Lot/5280/
> The Godseys

Appendix: The Casts

Cast of *Spencer's Mountain*

Olivia Spencer	Maureen O'Hara
Clay Spencer.	Henry Fonda
Grandpa Spencer	Donald Crisp
Grandma Spencer	Lillian Bronson
Clayboy Spencer.	James MacArthur
Becky Spencer	Veronica Cartwright
Preacher Goodman	Wally Cox
Claris Coleman	Mimsy Farmer
Percy Cook.	Dub Taylor
Mother Ida	Hope Summers
Col. Coleman	Hayden Rorke
Mr. John.	Ken Mayer
Miss Parker.	Virginia Gregg
Dr. Campbell	Whit Bissell
Minni-Cora Cook	Kathy Bennett
College Secretary	Bronwyn Fitzsimmons

Cast of *The Homecoming*

Olivia Walton	Patricia Neal
John Walton	Andrew Duggan
Grandpa Walton	Edgar Burgen
Grandma Walton	Ellen Corby
John-Boy Walton.	Richard Thomas
Jason Walton	Jon Walmsley
Mary Ellen Walton	Judy Norton
Erin Walton	Mary McDonough

Ben Walton . . . . Eric Scott
Jim-Bob Walton . . . . David Harper
Elizabeth Walton . . . . Kami Cotler
Sheriff Ep Bridges . . . . David Huddleston
Ike Godsey . . . . Woodrow Parfrey
Emily Baldwin . . . . Dorothy Stickney
Mamie Baldwin . . . . Josephine Hutchinson
Charlie Snead . . . . William Windom
Hawthorne Dooley . . . . Cleavon Little
City Lady . . . . Sally Chamberlin

Cast of *The Waltons*

The Walton Family

John Walton . . . . Ralph Waite
Olivia Walton . . . . Michael Learned
Zebulon Walton . . . . Will Geer
Esther Walton . . . . Ellen Corby
John-Boy Walton . . . . Richard Thomas 1972–77
John-Boy Walton . . . . Robert Wightman 1979–81
Jason Walton . . . . Jon Walmsley
Mary Ellen Walton Willard Jones . . . . Judy Norton
Ben Walton . . . . Eric Scott
Erin Walton . . . . Mary McDonough
Jim-Bob Walton . . . . David Harper
Elizabeth Walton . . . . Kami Cotler

Supporting Cast

Toni Hazelton Walton . . . . Lisa Harrison
Cindy Brunson Walton . . . . Leslie Winston
Dr. Curtis Willard . . . . Tom Bower
John Curtis Willard . . . . Marshall/Michael Reed
Martha Corinne Walton . . . . Beulah Bondi
Boone Walton . . . . Morgan Woodward
Wade Walton . . . . Richard Hatch
Ike Godsey . . . . Joe Conley
Corabeth Walton Godsey . . . . Ronnie Claire Edwards
Aimee Louise Godsey . . . . Rachel Longaker
Miss Mamie Baldwin . . . . Helen Kleeb
Miss Emily Baldwin . . . . Mary Jackson
Drew Cutler . . . . Tony Becker
Sheriff Ep Bridges . . . . John Crawford

Sara Griffith	Lynn Carlin
Homer Lee Baldwin	Denver Pyle
Polonius Baldwin	Iggie Wolfington
Verdie Grant Foster	Lynn Hamilton
Harley Foster	Hal Williams
Zuleika Dunbar	Pearl Shear
Dr. David Spencer	Robert Merritt Woods
Buck Vernon	Barry Cahill
Rev. Matthew Fordwick	John Ritter
Rosemary Hunter Fordwick	Mariclare Costello
Yancy Tucker	Robert Donner
G. W. Haines	David Doremus
Fannie Tatum	Sheila Allen
Flossie Brimmer	Nora Marlowe
Horace Brimley	Wilford A. Brimley
Bobby Bigelow	Mayf Nutter
Maud Gormley	Merie Earle
Rev. Hank Buchanan	Peter Fox
Rev. Tom Marshall	Kip Niven
Stanley Perkins	William Schallert
Daisey Garner	Deirdre Lenihan
Ashley Longworth Jr.	Jonathan Frakes
Arlington "Jonesy" Jones	Richard Gilliand
Rose Burton	Peggy Rea
Serena Burton	Martha Nix
Jeffrey Burton	Keith Mitchell
Martha Rose	Cindy Eilbacher
Marcia Woolery	Tami Bula
Dr. Vance	Victor Izay
Chad Marshall	Michael O'Keefe
Patsy Brimmer	Debbie Gunn
Paul Matthews Northridge	Morgan Stevens
J. D. Pickett	Lewis Arquette

Guest Stars (A Partial Listing)

Ellen Geer	Eva Mann, "The Ceremony"
David Huddleston	A. J. Covington, "The Literary Man"
Pippa Scott	Alvira Drummond, "The Actress"
Sian Barbara Allen	Jenny Pendleton "The Love Story"
Eduard Franz	Cody Nelson, "The Courtship"
Ned Beatty	Curtis Norton, "The Bicycle"
Sissy Spacek	Sarah Simmonds, "The Townie"
Dennis Dugan	Stuart Lee, "The Theft"
Peter Donat	Oscar Cockrell, "The Prize"

Michael McGreevey . . . . Hobie, "The Braggart"
Paul Michael Glaser . . . . Todd Cooper, "The Air-Mail Man"
Noah Beery . . . . Mr. Harnan, "The Heritage"
Ron Howard . . . . Seth Turner, "The Gift"
Victor French . . . . Curtis Norton, "The Fulfillment"
Ed Lauter . . . . Mr. Rudge, "The Car"
Paul Fix . . . . Lucas Avery, "The Conflict"
Lawrence Dobkin . . . . Professor Ghote, "The First Day"
Kathleen Quinlan . . . . Selina Linville, "The Thoroughbred"
Richard Masur . . . . Tom Povich, "The System"
Linda Purl . . . . Alicia, "The Spoilers"
Charles Haid . . . . Fred, "The Marathon"
Gerald McRaney . . . . Tim Collins, "The Book"
Madge Sinclair . . . . Minnie Doze, "The Visitor"
Rance Howard . . . . Dr. McIvers, "The Birthday"
Don Berry . . . . Deputy Sheriff, "The Birthday
Darleen Carr . . . . Sis Bradford, "The Beguiled"
Erin Moran . . . . Sally Ann Harper, "The Song"
Virginia Gregg . . . . Ada Corley, "The Ordeal"
Cleavon Little . . . . James Travis Clark, "The Fighter"
George Dzundza . . . . A. J. Covington, "The Abdication"
Abby Dalton . . . . Stella Lewis, "The Test"
Walter Brooke . . . . Mr. Johnson, "The Fledgling"
Kathleen Quinlan . . . . Selina Linville, "The Collision"
Merle Haggard . . . . Red Turner, "The Comeback"
Donald Moffatt . . . . Mr. Morgan, "John's Crossroads"
Bettye Ackerman . . . . Belle Becker, "The Achievement"
Louise Latham . . . . Aunt Kate, "The Milestone"
Lloyd Nolan . . . . Cyrus Guthrie, "The Return"
Jeanette Nolan . . . . Sister Scholastica, "The Calling"
Dean Jagger . . . . Professor Bowen, "Founder's Day"

Index

Nolan, Jeanette, 214
Nolan, Lloyd, 214
Norris, Patty, 47
Norton, Judy, 49, 62, 69,
 94–95, 114, 136, 165,
 211–212
Nutter, Mayf, 213

*O*akland Raiders, 39
O'Connor, John J., 58
O'Hara, Maureen, 37–38,
 211

*P*acker, Juliet Law,
 150–151, 153–154,
 157, 162–163, 168,
 170–171, 176, 178, 186
Paley, William, 55, 60
Palfrey, Woody, 48
Palm Springs Weekend, 40
Parfrey, Woodrow, 212
Parker, William, 158, 169
PBS, 210
Peabody Award, 10, 64
Perry, Joyce, 145
Peterson, Rod, 112, 117,
 120, 123, 125, 129,
 132–133, 139–140,
 142–143, 146, 148,
 159, 161, 171–172,
 186–187
Philips, Lee, 77, 81–82,
 93, 95, 108, 183
Phillips, Dorothy, 203, 209
Pirosh, Robert, 151, 154,
 159, 164, 168, 172,
 175
Polifroni, Pam, 45, 48

Porter, Irene, 70, 72, 203,
 208
Power, Katharyn, 133
Pringle, Joan, 152
Pugh, Madelyn, 174
Purl, Linda, 133, 214
Pyle, Denver, 213

*Q*uinlan, Kathleen, 214

*R*adio City Music Hall,
 21, 38
Radnitz, Robert, 40
*Raleigh News and
 Observer,* 203
Raschella, Carole, 141
Raschella, Michael, 141
Rea, Peggy, 162, 170, 174,
 177, 179–180, 213
Red Sky at Morning, 45
Redgrave, Sir Michael, 39
Reed, Marshall, 212
Reed, Michael, 212
Religious Public Relations
 Council, 9
Rich, Lee, 44, 57, 59
*Richmond Times
 Dispatch,* 20
Richmond, University of,
 21–23, 25, 64, 199
Ritter, John, 74, 213
Robinson, Matt, 114
Rockettes, 28
Rockfish River, 7, 199–200
Rockfish, Virginia, 7, 105,
 119, 135, 159, 182,
 199–200
Roosevelt, Franklin, 135
Roots, 83

Rorke, Hayden, 211
Rosebrook, Jeb, 81, 100,
 103–104, 149–150
Rupert, Michael, 75
Russnow, Michael, 98, 102,
 115

*S*alter, Susie, 33
Sanford and Son, 83, 89
Savage, Paul, 78–79, 82,
 153
Sayres, Julie, 188–189
Schell, Maximilian, 39
Schuyler Baptist Church, 7
Schuyler Community
 Center, 192
Schuyler, Virginia, 3–4, 7,
 18, 21–22, 24, 41, 171,
 185, 191–193,
 195–196, 198, 201,
 205, 207, 209, 222
Schwartz, Roseblanche, 44
Scott, Eric, 49–50, 62, 69,
 73, 76, 127, 129, 166,
 212
Scott, Joan, 114, 138
Scott, Pippa, 214
Seek, Christine, 106
Selner, Dave, 209
Senensky, Ralph, 89–90,
 96–97, 100–101,
 104–105, 108, 123,
 126–127, 138–139,
 146, 148, 151
Serling, Rod, 28, 31
Shallert, William, 180
Shea, Jack, 79, 84, 88, 91,
 95, 104, 106–107
Shear, Pearl, 213
Sheldon, James, 177, 179

Shell, Duane, 72, 96, 127, 136, 149, 178
Sherman, Vincent, 65, 76, 80, 82
Siegel, Lionel E., 95, 99
Silberman, Jim, 34, 44
Silverman, Freddie, 45
Simmons, Jean, 39
Sinclair, Madge, 214
Sipes, Marilyn, 100
Skelton, Red, 28
Skyline Drive, 8, 100
Slezak, Walter, 39
Smith, Cecil, 64
Smith, Claris Ross, 30
Smith, Mark, 30
Smithsonian Institution, 52
Sound of Music, The, 85
Spacek, Sissy, 85, 214
Spear, Stephen, 88
Stark, Sheldon, 89
Starsky and Hutch, 95
Steiner, Max, 38
Stevens, Morgan, 213
Stewart, Larry, 157
Stickney, Dorothy, 48–49, 212
Sudlow, Sarah, 119
Summers, Hope, 211
Sweeney, Bob, 175

*T*aylor, Dub, 211
Temptation Island, 205
Thaw, Mort, 93
Theater Guild on the Air, 30, 222
They Shoot Horses, Don't They?, 104
Thomas, Richard, viii–xi, xvi, 45, 47–48, 56–57,

62, 64, 74, 98, 100, 105, 109, 118, 121, 126, 131, 135–136, 188, 211–212
Timmons, Kirby, 120
To Kill a Mockingbird, 35
Today Show, 30
Toledo Blade, 59
Torrey, Allen, 205
Twentieth Century Fox, 7, 44, 104
Twilight Zone, The, 31–32, 40, 222

*U*lman, Dan, 166
United States Steel Hour, The, 30
Upstairs, Downstairs, 135

*V*an Haren, Alex and Marca, 203, 209
Virginia Press Association, 64
Virginia Stone Company, 196
Virginia, University of, 85, 100, 158

*W*agon Train, 39
Waite, Ralph, 57–58, 61–62, 71, 79, 91–92, 98–99, 106, 109–110, 112, 119, 123, 132, 138, 141–144, 151, 160, 166, 169, 188, 192, 212
Wallengren, E. F., 155, 157, 161, 164–165, 169, 173, 175, 179

Walmsley, Jon, 48, 62, 69, 74, 86, 97, 99, 113, 117, 123, 133, 145, 148, 177, 211–212
Walton's Friendship Society, 70, 72
Walton's Mountain Museum, 191–201, 207, 208
Waltons International Fan Club, 67, 192, 208
Warner Brothers, 32, 36, 39, 74, 79, 129
Watkins, Linda, 87
Wayne, John, 97
Webster, Nick, 98
Welch, William, 75
Wellman, Cissy, 90
West, Paul, 113–114, 116, 124, 131, 135, 145
Weverka, Robert, 111
Wheeler, David, 159
Whitaker, Claire (Peterson), 112, 117–118, 120, 123–125, 129, 132–133, 139–140, 142–144, 146–147, 148, 159, 160–161, 171–172, 175, 186–187
White, Andy, 111, 113, 123, 131, 135, 137, 140
Wightman, Robert, 212
Williams, Hal, 89, 213
Williams, John, 39
Winant, Ethel, 45
Windom, William, 48, 212
Winston, Leslie, 166–167, 187, 212

About the Authors

Earl Hamner is best known as the creator and producer of the Emmy Award–winning television series *The Waltons*. The producer of *Falcon Crest* and other television series, he has also written for *The Twilight Zone, CBS Playhouse,* and *Theater Guild on the Air.* His seven best-selling books include *Spencer's Mountain, The Homecoming, You Can't Get There from Here,* and *The Avocado Drive Zoo.* He lives in Studio City, California. **Ralph Giffin** is president of Blue Ridge Publications in Ocean Pines, Maryland.